I have been a Jew during Fascism, a Jew during Communism, a rebel defeated in an uprising, a refugee among the free, and a have-not amid plenty.

This book contains over 60 stories that range from my youth in Hungary, the ordeal of a death march and concentration camps, the oppression of the Communist dictatorship, the promise and defeat of the Hungarian Revolution and, finally, my American years.

I am a physician and an artist. Medicine is an art as, indeed, is living. Art and medicine are two consequences of the same desire—to sustain life.

Six values guide my life:

1. **The value of compassion.** From my Holocaust experience I ask what those silent, slaughtered millions would ask of us now? Hatred and revenge—the very qualities that led to their demise? Not likely. I believe they would want us to have understanding, compassion, and love.
2. **The value of equal treatment.** A double standard is the biggest threat to civilization.
3. **The value of children.** Nothing is more important than the moral and intellectual education of our future generations.
4. **The value of humor.** I take humor seriously.
5. **The value of suffering.** Suffering has made me appreciate how precious life is. Hardship has made every minute, every slice of bread, more enjoyable and meaningful.
6. **The value of remaining humane even in inhumane circumstances.**

The stories in this book are short and long, historical and philosophical, funny and solemn, humane and barbaric, realistic and sentimental. Yet each story portrays the presence or absence of my six guiding values.

Fisch Stories

Reflections on Life, Liberty, and the Pursuit of Happiness

Robert O. Fisch

to Peter 1/27/10

with friendship wishing

you a great life.

Ronald O. Fi—

ISBN 978-0-9679746-1-3

Contents

Introduction ix

Childhood and
Concentration Camps (1925–1945) 3

After the War (1945–1956) 21

American Years (1957–) 45

Musings about Human Nature
and Society 73

Musings about Life and Spirit 95
Holiday Gifts 126

Epilogue 149

In memory of
my beloved parents, Zoltán and Irén Fisch,
and my dear governess, Anna Tátrai
To my daughter, Alex, my wife, Karen, and my friends,
with love

Introduction

"I wish you an interesting life" go the words of an ancient Chinese curse. My life has been interesting: I have been a Jew during Fascism, a bourgeois under the Communists, a rebel defeated in an uprising, a refugee among the free, and a have-nothing amid plenty. And I had to take a high-school examination 12 years after receiving a medical diploma. This means I have unlimited subject matter, all of which I have viewed through the lens of my own eye and mind. The experiences of life—faith, injustice, joy, sadness, childhood, growing up, parenthood, health, illness, love, hate, death—are much the same for all of us; the angles from which we see and respond to them are what make the difference.

One recurrent issue in my life has been the double standard. During all the periods of my life the issue of most concern—for many different reasons and in many circumstances—has been ignorance of the Golden Rule. Many people do not treat others as they wish to be treated themselves. The Golden Rule may prove my primary subject—it is what I have been fighting for.

There may be a billion universes. We know that "our" universe contains billions of galaxies, each with billions of stars, each star surrounded by many planets, most of them lifeless, and we humans are constantly searching for signals (radio, infrared, visible light, ultraviolet, X-rays, gamma rays) from outer space. Indeed, with great expense and effort, we send signals to the vast universe in the hope that there are others who might listen to us or want us to listen to them. Although family members, neighbors, tribes, countries, nations, religions, and races for millennia have not been able to understand or communicate well with each other (to say the least), we turn to outer space with elaborate telescopes; we try to communicate with some extraterrestrial intelligence what we cannot achieve within and among ourselves.

Our need to express ourselves is undoubtedly greater than our need to listen. We want to amplify our thoughts and feelings by expressing them in words; in fact, we may wish for an echo more than for anything else.

I am no exception. I write to communicate, to share the feelings, experiences, and thoughts that have been accumulating within during my many years and happenings. My main hope is that this book will make some contribution toward a kinder world and a better future for the children of today.

In the concentration camps we rarely spoke. Neither death nor survival was a topic of our limited conversation. But food! In our cloud of hunger, thinking about food was the silver lining.

And when we lived under the suppressive Communist system, our jokes ridiculing the political system and its leaders made it possible to endure dismal, hopeless days. In sadness, humor provided hope.

Hungarians have a peculiar personality: we enjoy ourselves and we cry at the same time. Liszt's music, for instance, alternates happy (up) melodies with sad (down) ones. My moods and, in fact, my whole life, have followed a similar pattern. Individual episodes and moments, ups and downs, together weave the whole fabric of my life's flow. Each moment is a piece of the mosaic of life.

Childhood and Concentration Camps

(1925–1945)

Family Tree

Once I was invited to the home of a South American doctor who displayed his family tree on the wall. He proudly showed me that one of his ancestors was among the first conquerors who traveled to the New World from Spain. Fortunately, I do not have any information about my family tree. I am convinced that I am much better off not knowing too much about my ancestors. From the time my ancient ancestors were chased from their land a few thousand years ago, the only heritage they carried—besides a few books—was suffering and misery.

My grandfather was 12 years old when he left a little Polish village alone (I assume the reason was poverty, but I don't know the details) and walked barefoot first to Russia, later to Budapest. There he sold water from a tin cup in an amusement park. His more adventurous older brothers reached Paris and New York, and although they lacked both food and education, all were successful in their new countries.

After my grandfather went into the poultry business and became a wealthy man, he was offered the title of baron in return for a substantial amount of money. He refused, saying, "Who would buy a chicken from Baron Fisch?"

5

My mother had to leave her home in Zenta (then in Hungary now in Yugoslavia) when she was 15 years old, to earn a living. She worked six days a week, 14 hours a day. Because she was deprived of an education, she provided my brother and me with private teachers, even for music and religion. After World War II, she went at age 58 to Israel, where worked helping elderly women. She emigrated from Israel to the United States when she was 66 and began working again, within two weeks of her arrival. She worked until she died at 86, never accepting a penny from her engineer and doctor sons. From her I learned determination, endurance, and responsibility.

My father enjoyed everything life could offer: music, food, theater, playing dominoes, and so forth. He and my mother had a shop that sold poultry and game. He was an exceptionally good person, and he helped so many needy people, mostly children in orphanages. In 1944, when he was 53 years old, Hungarian Nazis took him to a Hungarian concentration camp near the German border. A survivor told me that on the way he gave his food away, saying "I have enough."

Before he died in the camp, my father's last words were: "If people can do such things to each other, life is not worth living!" He was so respected that he was the only one not buried in a separate, not a common, grave. He taught me love, laughter, and compassion.

In 1956, I also participated in the Hungarian Revolution as a physician, treating injured revolutionaries as well as Russian and Hungarian soldiers, helping to save hundreds of lives. In the year 2000 the Hungarian government awarded me knighthood for my role as a freedom fighter. In my family, nobility wasn't inherited; it was inherent.

The Violinist

Hungarian goose liver is second only to that of the French. It is made by force-feeding geese, usually with corn. My mother, who was in the poultry business, believed in force-feeding geese but also in force-feeding me—at mealtime and with violin practice as well. I knew the Jews had suffered since the Diaspora, but I had never heard of the violin being used as an instrument of torture.

Shortly after my music teacher resigned because of my disagreeable personality and complete lack of musical promise, my father met a professional violinist, a refugee from Romania. The violinist needed a tuxedo to perform in an orchestra, so my father bought him one. In gratitude he gave us a violin and offered to become my violin teacher.

I was a religious child, but resuming my violin lessons with a Romanian refugee was not in my prayers. He came punctually twice a week for one-hour lessons. I had no choice but to accept punishment for my ancestors' sins and practice the violin every day as prescribed.

One day my teacher did not show up. Soon after that, two men came to see my father. They were from Interpol, and they were looking for the "violinist," who turned out to be a notorious criminal and multiple murderer. Suddenly I understood that the violinist and I had had a kind of telepathy. Whenever he gave me a lesson, I started thinking about murder.

My Surgery

One autumn evening in 1942, two bombs dropped on Budapest, starting Hungary's involvement in World War II. I was 17 years old and a year from graduation.

Our apartment had four tall double windows. We were instructed to keep our outer windows open during air raids and to tape paper on the inside windows to block debris.

I had to really stretch my right arm to tape the paper to the top of each window. I was proud of my achievement. When my father came home, I showed him my work, and he said, "I have a feeling this will cost me more than if I had hired workers from Vienna." He was right. A week later I collapsed with a high fever, and our family doctor diagnosed a severe inflammation of my right-arm axillary glands. Some blood vessels had ruptured and become infected.

There were no antibiotics, and surgery could not prevent sepsis or the myocarditis that followed. I was in critical condition. Amputation was considered. My wonderful nanny, Anna, sat by my bed every day. During the operation the surgeon had inserted tampons for drainage. During my recovery he had to cut through my skin to get them out. It was extremely painful. The second time this happened I asked for a pain reliever and got an injection. Very quickly I felt strange and thought the end was coming. I told Anna I was going to die. She cried. But I felt light, as if I were floating in air. I was not scared, only relieved that my suffering would be over soon.

I was ecstatic when the orderly rolled me to the treatment room. I told him that we all have to face death and should not be afraid of it. When the surgeon cut through the skin, I was delighted. My euphoria lasted for hours. I've never experienced anything like that in my life and have never felt closer to heaven.

When my family doctor arrived, he saw my reaction and was furious that I had received morphine. He said if I had another injection I could become addicted. It did not happen again. But I understand why so many people choose narcotics and knowingly face the detrimental consequences. The only reasonable way to avoid addiction is to refrain from trying the drugs.

A Dog Story: Fricike

The whole thing started June 4, 1944, in Vác, city north of Budapest. I was 19 years old. The Nazis demanded that every Jewish man from 18 to 48 years of age be registered for forced labor. We were facing an unknown future and most likely our end.

At dawn 280 of us walked toward the railroad station. The city was asleep, and the noise of our hobnailed boots on the cobblestones sounded ominously of outcasts. We walked in desperation, realizing we were unwanted or worse. Suddenly a little stray dog, an outcast like us, joined us. Eventually we were pushed into cattle cars, and one of us lifted in that miserable little animal.

When we arrived at our destination in eastern Hungary, we were assigned to a bridge-building military unit and had to wear yellow armbands. We named the little dog Fricike and tied a yellow ribbon on his left leg, so he became an official member of our unit. He certainly was not intimidated like the rest of us. He barked at our guards whenever he encountered them.

Every morning he went out from the barracks with us and roamed the area while we worked at building bridges. This involved, among other things, digging out unexploded bombs. It was all physical labor, but at least that meant we were fed well. At night when we returned from work, Fricike was already waiting for us. In January

1945, we started on a forced death march toward the German border because the Nazis did not want us to be liberated. Fricike walked with us faithfully. His presence meant more to us than ever.

Before we reached the border, the Hungarian military diverted 80 of us to be crammed into cattle cars. At the border the train stopped, and our captors threw in a loaf of bread, compliments of our country. When Fricike jumped out to answer his bodily demands (something denied to us), the Germans ordered the doors closed. We pleaded with them in vain to hand us the dog, but they locked the doors. Fricike was left behind. Everyone became quiet, and when I looked around I saw faces full of bitterness and fear. Now we were all alone in our suffering.

Shortly thereafter our death march resumed, and within a few months two-thirds of us had been felled by bullets or hunger during our trek through the Alps. We had marched more hundreds of miles, through Austria to the Mauthausen concentration camp, and then to our final destination, a death camp in Gunskirchen.

During long stretches of the march, we did not receive any food or water. Then one day I suddenly saw Fricike walking in the line ahead of us. He was a skeleton, like each of us, skin and bones, and he barley crawled. We understood that this bony little creature shared our faith. We walked, drawing renewed strength from his presence, faithfulness, and solidarity.

What happened to Fricike? I do not know. Maybe he starved or was shot, like many of us. Or maybe he survived. But he never left us. Fricike touched us then. He touches me still.

Spitfires

Once for a few hours in February 1945, the Germans put us in cattle cars to move us away from the approaching Russian army. Suddenly the train stopped, and we were ordered to evacuate the cars. The railroad was among trees on the top of a hill. On the road below we saw a German truck convoy. Suddenly British Spitfires started strafing the convoy. They were flying right above us, so low that they seemed to touch the trees. Oh, what a sight that was! I was so excited that I jumped for joy. I could see the liberators fighting for our freedom, and they were almost within reach. But in the midst of my glee, a guard beat me with his gunstock until I collapsed.

Freedom was much farther away than a few feet above our heads.

Bean Soup

In the winter of 1945 thousands of emaciated skeletons walked for nearly three months through the Alps, sometimes going four or five days without food or water. Those who could not walk any farther were shot. In April we had the first "roof" over our heads in the concentration camp of Mauthausen. Actually the roof was a large circus-like tent, but it seemed to be an improvement.

Certainly it would have been naive to believe that our new accommodations meant the overall quality of other essentials would improve, even a bit. A small piece of moldy green bread and a cup of coffee comprised our daily food allowance. This so-called "comfort" lasted only a few days, until we continued the march towards our final destination: the Death Camp of Gunskirchen. But this brief respite, during which we did not have to go anywhere or do anything, was an unusual opportunity to communicate with one another. The major subject of our limited conversations was food. We cared about nothing else, and we had neither the interest in nor the energy for anything else.

German cartoons portrayed images of Jews as rich, fat, well-dressed bankers smoking big cigars. The reality was another story. Most of my fellow prisoners were simple, poor hard-working adults with families. One of them, like me, was 19 years old. Once he turned to me and asked, "Tell me, if someone went to a restaurant, could he order as much bean soup as he wished?" He never found out.

Fifty Years Later

Gunskirchen was a death camp, one of the many sub-camps of Mauthausen concentration camp. Its only purpose was to liquidate Jewish prisoners. More than 18,000—mostly Hungarians, like me—had arrived there from Mauthausen. On May 4, 1945, the eve of my liberation, I was 19 years old and extremely weak. When my American liberators came, I had to crawl over the barracks threshold to meet them.

The American soldier who found me asked, "Why?"

I told him, "Because I am a Jew."

They couldn't believe their eyes. They couldn't believe our stories. Who could? Later in the American camp I wrote the following poem:

> Tormented by the memory of the past,
> Being in hell, where the living were burned alive,
> Now I am free, begging, on my knees,
> Use my blood, for love.

In April 1995, I received an invitation to the 50th anniversary celebration of the liberation of Gunskirchen and Mauthausen. Members of the 71st Infantry Division of the U.S. Third Army, as well as some of the survivors, would be there. Although I had very short notice, I felt I had to go because it would give me an opportunity to thank the American soldiers for saving my life. In reality my liberation was my rebirth. According to an old Jewish custom, a person who survives a serious sickness or life-threatening situation chooses a new name for his new life. (I wonder how much confusion this causes in the heavenly register!)

I arrived in Linz, Austria, on the evening of May 3. The next morning, after sleeping in a comfortable hotel and eating a good breakfast, I went by car to the Gunskirchen campsite in the middle of a forest. It was a warm, sunny day—quite a contrast from my first arrival in the rain after the five-day march from Mauthausen. Deprived of food and water, we had been increasingly unable to walk. SS Germans put the weak on pallets rigged to horses. They threw the exhausted directly into open graves and shot them.

The Gunskirchen campsite is now private property, and it was difficult for me to imagine later that those peaceful woods were the site of the incomprehensible events of a half-century before. Oddly, I felt nothing special. As a matter of fact, I was unable to find anything remaining from or reminiscent of the horrifying past. When the others arrived, they showed me the temporary markers indicating the location of the barracks.

Dale Speckman, a private in 1945, had been the first liberator to reach us. He came upon Gunskirchen accidentally; he had been lost in the forest when he noticed a terrible smell that led him to the camp, the smell of excrement and dead bodies. Now more than 80 years old, he cried like a child as he came to the markers and placed a yellow-star wreath at the site.

That was the point at which this innocent-looking site, the last place on earth for thousands of people, finally touched me. The presence of the American Honor Guard reminded me of the enormous sacrifices of the people of the United States during the war. I shall never forget, nor should the world. I am privileged to be an American today.

Back in Gunskirchen's community hall, high-school students performed Israeli dances and songs for a meeting of the townspeople and their visitors. It was a fine example of goodwill. Suddenly, a woman from the audience ran up to the microphone, held up a picture, and asked in three languages—English, German, and Hungarian—whether anyone recognized the man in the photo. She was still searching for her father, 50 years after he had disappeared.

A Hungarian survivor sitting near me showed me an old silver pocket watch. "You know, Dr. Fisch, this watch belonged my father. You see his name is engraved inside the lid. We lived in Székesfehérvár. He disappeared, and we never found out what happened to him. My brother became a watchmaker and moved far away. Seven years after the war, a man brought a watch in for repair. When my brother opened the cover, he saw his father's engraved name. He asked the man where he got the watch, but he ran out of the shop and disappeared."

The next day we went to Mauthausen, for seven years one of the most feared concentration camps. Built in 1938 for criminals, it was later used for political prisoners—that is, anyone who was considered an enemy of the Third

Reich. Now it is a museum with meticulous documentation of the more than 120,000 men, women, and children from all over Europe—and soldiers from England and America—whom the Nazis killed there. I learned that the liberators found the following words written in blood on the wall of Mauthausen's jail (imagine a jail in a concentration camp!): "If there is a God, He must be on His knees, begging my forgiveness."

Our group included a survivor, now a successful businessman in the United States, who wished never to return to the camp. But one day he decided to show his children and grandchildren the place where he had lost his family and his youth. At the gate to Mauthausen, the guard asked him for an entry fee of 10 schillings. He became so enraged at being asked to pay to re-enter the hell of his past that he hit the guard and went in. Soon he was arrested and taken before a judge. But the judge apologized to him and promised that from then on no one who had ever been a prisoner at Mauthausen would be asked to pay an entrance fee. There is now a sign to this effect at the entrance.

Today the Nazi symbol and the sign "Arbeit Macht Frei" are gone from the main gate. I was a prisoner there for only four days, though it seemed much longer.

Fifty years later I watched as Thomas Klestil, the president of Austria, lay a wreath on a memorial inscribed: "May the living learn from the fate of the dead." I thanked him. Walking in the peaceful green pastures dotted with small, simple crosses and Stars of David, I could barely comprehend the magnitude of the brutality and misery that had occurred here.

When I returned to America, I received a letter from the students I had met in Gunskirchen. They wrote that they had grown up in peace and prosperity. They had learned about the death march, the camps, and the atrocities committed against the Jewish prisoners. These adults of tomorrow said, "We want to do everything we can to ensure that nothing like that ever happens again."

As the Jewish prayer says, "Thank God for letting me live to this day."

What Would You Do?

Two thousand Russians managed to escape from the Mauthausen concentration camp on February 12, 1945. The Nazis hunted down and killed all but eight of them.

Can you imagine escaping over a three-meter-high wall topped by electrified barbed wires, then 18-feet beyond it? You must disarm the tower guard, turn off the electricity, climb over the wall and wire, and, though you are weak from extreme malnourishment when you reach the top of the wall, you must jump down from a height of five meters.

By the time they got that far, most of the captives could go no farther. The sirens screamed, the SS guards from inside and out closed in with dogs and machine guns; very few prisoners reached the edge of village. I saw the documents of a family whose father hid one of the prisoners. The father first had to let the escapee in, then helped him undress, gave him a shower and some clothes, burned the old ones (which smelled bad and were infested with lice), fed him, and hid him. The SS guards repeatedly searched each house from basement to attic. The family members were scared to death. If they found a hidden prisoner, the guards would kill every member of every household that helped the prisoners and pile their bodies in the village square.

During my "death" march, someone occasionally ran out with a glass of water as we passed. What a blessing that was! I wonder what I would have done if I had lived close to where—day after day, month after month—thousands of hungry and thirsty people walked past my house. Even if there had been no risk and plenty of food (neither of which was the case), even with good intentions, how often or for how long would I (or anyone) have run in and out and helped? How many of us would risk our own lives and the lives of our families to save a stranger, an enemy?

The Germans (fathers, husbands, and sons) had fought against the Russians. Only eight of the Russians trying to escape Mauthausen were saved. Maybe the issue is not that the Germans were bad, but that very few people are good.

After the War

(1945–1956)

Between Two Points

I was never good at mathematics, but I know the established rule that the shortest distance between two points is a straight line.

After the war, we who were liberated hoped to find some member of our families, or even our homes, and we started to go in the direction of our countries.

But some with the same purpose headed in the opposite direction, so as to avoid the crowd. They arrived home much sooner than the rest of us. That is when I learned the importance of taking risks and not following the sheep-like majority. The straight line may be the shortest distance between two points, but it is neither necessarily the fastest nor the best route.

Under Communism

When I returned to Budapest after the war, I saw that the destruction was not restricted to buildings. People and families were also in ruins. But life could not and did not stop, and gradually everyone started to adapt to a new way of life.

Owing to the poor health and lack of foresight of President Roosevelt, Hungary and the rest of Eastern Europe were to be managed (or more precisely, ruled) by the Soviet Union. This inevitably led to the gradual and meticulously planned takeover by the Communists of industry, land, and private property. Again, personal freedom became a thing of the past.

The Communists forced people not only to blindly follow Marxist-Leninist-Stalinist doctrines but also to deny their own backgrounds, friends, and moral values. The government at first nationalized a few large industrial complexes, but gradually worked its way down to the smaller companies and then to individual businesses and individuals. But if the rights of even a single individual can be denied, then no one's rights are secure. And if whole companies could be taken away, then I couldn't even safely call my pants my own.

I was asked to join the Communist Party. Positions, opportunities, and other doors would "open" to me. I had no difficulty in saying no, even knowing the inevitable consequences. Having been a victim of suppression in the previous regime, I was not now willing to become a suppressor myself.

Besides, I had seen the Russians in action. After the war, when the Americans escorted us Jews by train to the Russian Zone in Austria, Russian soldiers stole everything they could from us, as little as it was. When the train arrived in Austria, the Russian officer who met us spat and walked away from skeletal survivors whose language he couldn't understand.

I found shelter that evening in a burned-out building and fell asleep clinging to a pair of German boots to trade for food or money on the journey home. I awoke to two Russian soldiers trying to steal my boots. One of them aimed his submachine gun at me. Even though they were the only things I had, I decided it wasn't worth it to die in

Austria for a pair of German boots a month after surviving the war. So I let them take them.

A few days later, I was on a train at the Austria/Hungary border. The trains were crowded, with people sitting on top of the cars. Because I was so weak, I needed help to climb the steep steps into the car. We waited for more than 10 hours for the train to depart. Just before the train finally started, a group of drunken Russian soldiers boarded and threw me off the train onto the cement platform below.

These incidents were my introduction to Russian and Communist values and methods. It was only the beginning, of course. More—and much worse—came later. Arriving home at last, I learned that the Russians who "liberated" my mother had raped her when they found her in the village where she had hidden from the Nazis.

My Pilgrimage

For many Christians the destination of a pilgrimage is Bethlehem. For Jews it is the Wailing Wall in Jerusalem, and for Muslims it is Mecca. My pilgrimage always leads to my father's grave in Budapest's Jewish cemetery. It is far out of town, the last stop on the No. 28 streetcar. The cemetery, the largest Jewish graveyard in Hungary, opened in 1891.

My father died in a concentration camp in Hidegség, Hungary. As mentioned earlier, out of respect for his giving his food to other prisoners, he was buried in a single, separate grave. An eyewitness who knew the location of his grave told my mother about his death. Fortunately for us, the exhumation occurred before my mother and I arrived. The body was already in a sealed metal coffin, and we were presented a piece of cloth that I recognized as part of his coat. I remember stroking a nearby cow at the graveside. Long before my liberation I had lost all emotion. I didn't laugh; I didn't cry. When the first American came to the camp, I was too weak even to stand up. My physical status improved rapidly after I returned home, but my feelings remained a blank.

My father's funeral took place on a dark, cool afternoon in October 1945. He had taught me the importance of showing one's last respects by attending a person's funeral. But he did not receive that respect. The chief rabbi and cantor gave the service in the cemetery's synagogue, but only a handful attended. The ones who remained lived under constant fear of the drunken Russian soldiers who robbed men and molested women.

After the service we walked to a parcel that became the burial ground for many other martyrs. My father's grave was only partially dug. One of my mother's employees jumped in and completed the excavation. That was the first time I wept. All my father's love for life, compassion, and respect for other humans turned out to be a one-way street leading to a sorrowful end. His final grave was not even ready to receive him.

In 1949 a memorial to the Hungarian victims of the Holocaust was built next to my father's grave. There is a Remembrance Wall, before which stand a black marble sarcophagus and a menorah. Inscribed on the wall in Hebrew and Hungarian are words that translate: "They were killed by hatred; their memory is kept alive in love."

The memorial includes nine walls listing the locations of mass slaughter, along with 10,000 names of those who are known to have died, a fraction of the 600,000

Hungarian Jews killed. A small marble plaque represents the others—hundreds of thousands who disappeared and left no survivors. Each wall has a Bible quotation: One is: "I cried against brutality, but no one listened." Another is: "Even the stones weep."

Whenever I return to Budapest, I visit my father's grave on the first and last day of my trip. If my visit happens to be on a Saturday or on a holy day when the cemetery is closed, I find a way to boost myself over the high stone perimeter wall. Then I kiss the cold, hard marble of his grave marker, as I remember kissing his warm, gentle face. "Even death could not come between us."

Another Dog Story: Jacky

After WWII my mother had a food shop on a busy street in Budapest. The products she sold included game, such as deer and rabbit.

One of our neighbors owned the most beautiful champion German shepherd in Hungary, a dog named Jacky. My mother gave Jacky raw deer liver and other meats, which were scarce in those days. Jacky loved us, and when we saw him in the street or in our shop, he rubbed his beautiful head against us. When the Communists confiscated my mother's shop, Jacky's owner could no longer afford to feed him, and so he sold the dog to the Secret Police, who used Jacky to breed vicious dogs for guarding the border.

A few years later the son of Jacky's former owner and I were walking around the National Agriculture Fair held every September in Budapest. The AVO Secret Police were displaying their terrifying dogs there. Fastened with strong chains, they barked and snarled when anyone

walked by. We eyed them with trepidation. Then we saw
Jacky. We shouted his name, calling him to us. He recognized us immediately and, breaking his chain, ran to us
and happily rubbed his head against us, just as he had in
the past. His Secret Police handlers were astounded and
embarrassed.

As the Hungarian says, "You cannot make bacon from
a dog."

The Mining Barracks

During the Communist regime in Hungary, I was considered politically unreliable and so was prevented from pur-
suing a medical specialty and from working in Budapest.
Instead, the Party sent me to work as a general doctor in
a mining town called Tatabánya.

Every morning I got up at 5 A.M. and traveled by train
to Tatabánya, where I saw patients from 8 A.M. until
noon. In the early afternoons I made house calls on foot,
then returned to the clinic. I worked until 5 P.M., caught a
train back to Budapest, and arrived home around 9 P.M.
Every fourth night I stayed in Tatabánya and was on call
alone for a population of 80,000. At times I became so
exhausted that the phone fell out of my hand.

On Saturdays I worked until noon. And when I was
on call during the weekend, my work began again on
Monday morning as usual. That was socialized medicine, which today is a dream for many but for me was a
nightmare.

Despite the negatives, I loved taking care of the miners. Most of them lived in outdated houses and worked
very hard under dangerous circumstances.

One night I was called to a barracks where temporary

workers lived. Many of the workers there had dubious or criminal backgrounds, and they were kept isolated from the local miners. A policeman stood guard at the barracks entrance. I saw men with what looked like knife cuts. My patient that day was lying in a lower bunk. I examined him, diagnosed gastroenteritis, and gave him a prescription. Before I left, I asked him why the workers tolerated hooligans among them.

All of a sudden, a huge, half-naked, drunken man fell down from the top bunk. He stood up and came at me with a knife in his hand. I wasn't very strong and certainly not ready for a knife fight. As he came near me, I pushed him. Fortunately for me, he was drunk enough to fall down. I walked out quickly, before he had a chance to stand up again.

At the door I told the policeman that a drunk was stabbing men in the barracks.

He sprang to attention and saluted me. "Thank you, Mr. Doctor," he said as he turned and ran away.

One Liter

The miners were notoriously heavy drinkers, at least from 1954 to 1956, when I worked as a district doctor in the mining town in Hungary.

During my first week of work there, a young man came to see me. He told me he did not feel well and could not go to work. I was unable to not find anything wrong with him and, because of my lack of experience, I was unsure of what to do next. In desperation I told him that I would give him one day of sick leave if he would tell me the real reason he wanted to stay home. "Doctor," he said, "I drank 16 liters [about 4 gallons] of wine last night."

During the time I was a district doctor, my responsibilities included making house calls. That included giving intravenous injections to cardiac patients. These patients were supposed to restrict their fluid intake to a maximum of one liter a day.

I gave one such patient a daily injection for weeks. Near the end of his therapy one of his sons came to see me in my office. He expressed his thanks for his father's noticeable improvement after my daily visits.

Then he added, "And you know, doctor, it was good of you to restrict his liquid intake. He has followed your instructions and never drunk more than one liter of rum a day."

The Sourpuss

When I worked in Tatabánya, my role was to see to my patients' health and to determine whether they were well enough to work. If not, they required a medical certificate so as to be paid. This increased not only my administrative work but also the number of visits—from people who pretended to be sick because they did not want to work.

Among my patients was a single woman about 35 years old, who worked in an office and came to the clinic at least twice a week. Her unlimited complaints included symptoms extending to every part of her body. I couldn't make her well, and she was making me sick. My supervisor suggested I start an intimate relationship with her to relieve some of her misery. I refused on the basis that my salary did not justify such an excessive and painful responsibility.

One day a gracious, white-haired, elderly woman came

to see me. She was charming and good-natured. I recognized her name and asked whether she was related to the chronic complainer. She said the younger woman was her daughter. I've never had problems expressing my thoughts, and I asked her, "How could such a delightful woman have such a miserable creature for a daughter?"

She told me the following story: "My husband worked at the railway station. Everybody knew us. My daughter was engaged to a young man who also worked at the railroad company. The wedding day was set. We invited a few hundred friends to the church and then to our home to celebrate with dinner, gypsy music, and dancing.

"As is customary, we spent everything we had and more to make the wedding memorable. On the wedding day, the church was filled with guests and the bride was in a beautiful, long white dress. Bride and groom waited in separate rooms for the ceremony to begin. The organ music signaled the start of the ceremony, but nothing happened. After few minutes the guests became restless, and someone left to look for the groom. The window was open in the room where he had been waiting, and he was gone."

In those days people couldn't just move to another place if something embarrassing happened to them. So my constantly complaining patient stayed and was the laughing stock of the town for the rest of her life. And while I now sympathized with her, I wished I could jump out the window when she came to see me.

Fellini in Tihany

Tihany is a lovely village near Lake Balaton in Hungary. The lake is the largest in Eastern Europe and one of the most popular tourist places. My wonderful doctor friend,

Uncle Kazi, owned a villa near the lake. Uncle Kazi was the head of the Public Health Department during my exile to a mining town. He was the only person in a town of 80,000 who owned a car; although it was so old it looked more like a rusted sardine can.

Like so many other things during the Communist regime, his villa retained only a shadow of its original beauty. From the front of the garden, a lovely road lined with tall poplar trees led to the center of the town. Uncle Kazi and his wife, Ilike, spent each summer at the villa with their dogs, chickens, and ducks. They were such gentle people that the chickens were free to enter their house through the open doors. The animals were considered family members, and all died a natural death. They were never intended for the dinner table.

In about 1967, I visited my uncle and aunt. I didn't have much money. But the exchange rate for the dollar was high, so I carried a bundle of Hungarian currency worth little in any other country.

One day Kazi and Ilike drove me to the village. At the center was a square overlooking the with the spectacular Lake Balaton. The tourists brought there by huge Hungarian-made Icarus buses crowded the square.

After we had our coffee and pastries, Ilike started the car. Within minutes she managed to scrape the whole side of a nearby bus. When I called her attention to the mishap, she said, "It is nothing."

I saw the bus driver running after us. When he reached us, he said to Ilike, "Lady, don't you think we have to settle this?"

She replied that such a minor incident was not worth even discussing. And she was serious. I calculated that in U.S. terms such damage would cost several thousand dollars to repair. But I also knew that in the socialist "paradise" (that's what the Communists called it) things could be settled in a simpler way—with a bribe. When I told the bus driver I'd resolve the dispute, he asked me for a sizable amount of Hungarian currency, which was minuscule in dollars. (I knew he would keep it for himself, anyway.) I stepped out of the car and took the wad of bills from my pocket. Suddenly a puff of wind caught me off guard, and my money flew into the air like leaves from a tree. The people around us acted as if it were manna from heaven. They ran in crazy, happy excitement, trying to catch the floating money. It was like a scene from a Fellini movie: chaotic, noisy, and humorous. I never enjoyed losing my money more.

Two Episodes in Communist "Paradise"

In my first years of medical school at the University of Budapest, the different political parties pressured students to join. I established the Fisch Party and edited the *Fisch Journal*, both designed to ridicule the Communists. One spring, at a May 1 demonstration, the Communists produced a poster with a cartoon of President Truman with a snake around his neck. When they asked me to carry it, I refused. (The Party had co-opted the 18th-century workers' celebration of May Day—comparable to the American Labor Day—for its own purposes.)

"His soldiers liberated me," I told them. They put the poster on my back anyway, and after I threw it to the ground it tore in pieces and I walked away.

A few days later when I went to class, everyone moved away from me. The previous evening I had been condemned as an enemy to be shunned by the student body.

A Helpful Connection

My brother, who had attended school in Switzerland, told me he had a college friend who had become a leading physician in the Communist hierarchy as well as head of a division in the medical union. He might be able to help me become a specialist. So before my graduation from medical school, I went to the medical union office. When I asked the secretary to see him, she gave me a funny look and quickly left the room.

I felt that something was wrong, and I ran from the building. I later learned that my brother's friend had been arrested during a Communist purge and beaten to death. As a consequence of becoming suspect, I was prohibited from becoming a specialist, and after my graduation in 1953, I was sent to work as a general practitioner in the country.

Revolution in Hungary

We usually think of a revolution as a well-planned event carried out by a well-organized group. But the Hungarian Revolution was not like that at all.

On the evening of October 23, 1956, a cheerful crowd of students gathered in front of Budapest's main radio station, where the prime minister was to give a speech. The radio station was along a small, narrow street, and the students, hoping to block the entrance, had gathered there. Because there were so many students, the secret police sent in several units to protect the radio station. The ebullient students cheered the police.

I was attending a medical meeting nearby, but more fascinated by the demonstration, I joined the crowd. As a war "veteran," I was cautious and distrustful. I stayed close to a corner building across the street from the radio station, using it as a shield.

The students were as noisy as students anywhere, and their only intention was to prevent the prime minister from entering the radio station. They had no weapons; in Hungary at that time, only the police and military could have arms. At eight o'clock, the prime minister began his speech, broadcasting remotely from his office. And at eight o'clock, the secret police opened fire machine-gun fire on the students from the balcony of the radio station.

At first I thought, "What kind of system uses bullets against unarmed students?"

Next I rushed to the medical meeting to round up my fellow doctors to help the injured, whom we took to a nearby emergency clinic. The street fell silent as the uninjured took cover and waited. I went home.

The next morning when I looked out the window, I saw children—some as young as 12 years old—with guns. The secret police had asked the military for backup, but the Hungarian soldiers had joined with the students and given them weapons.

This astonishing development was the first crack in the massive wall of the system that had devoured entire nations, held a hundred million people behind the Iron Curtain, and constantly threatened the security of the rest of world. The revolution was unorthodox in all respects. The revolutionaries were not the suppressed classes but young people who had known no other system. Just as a seed breaks through the ground, instinctively seeking light, the young revolutionaries were searching for a freedom they had never experienced. The whole revolution lasted no more than 10 days (late October to November 4) but nevertheless cracked the wall.

At that time I was working with premature infants, but it seemed to me hypocritical to try to save a few tiny babies when children and young adults were being injured and killed. The next day I went to Péterfy Sándor Hospital, where I had received surgical and anesthesiology training, to rally a few people to find a way to transport the wounded. With the help of medical students, we broke into a government garage and stole cars to do so. Having, as it did, the only mobilized transportation system, the hospital became a center of the revolution.

Volunteers, many of whom were killed in doing so, drove wherever there was fighting and picked up the injured—revolutionaries and Russians alike. We undressed them in the hospital elevator and took them to the emergency room to identify blood type and start intravenous solutions before moving them immediately to surgery. For 24 hours a day we performed surgery. The surgeons were expedient and effective, but post-operative care and medications were limited, and mortality was high.

Some revolutionaries came to the hospital to try to identify their Communist opponents. I convinced them that the hospital had only one rule: to help the injured. After our patients recovered, what went on outside was their business.

A day after the defeat of the revolution (the Russians supposedly were leaving, though they came back in full force), a Russian colonel came to the hospital carrying a machine gun. He wanted to pick up the 160 injured Russian soldiers. At the entrance, I told him he had to put down his weapon, and he did. During his visit, Russian soldiers on the street below rounded up a group of rebels, holding them at gunpoint. When the colonel learned from the Russian patients how well they were treated in the hospital, he ordered that the rebels be let go.

Hundreds of Hungarian people waited patiently in line outside the hospital to donate blood. When their turns came, some gave money to buy medicine for the injured, even though they were poor and had been deprived of essentials for years.

Shop windows were broken. In a camera shop in which one camera could cost my six months' salary, the smashed window had a note taped across it: "We do not fight for cameras." None was taken.

A boy tried to take off a wristwatch from a dead body. Another boy shot him, saying, "That is not what we are fighting for."

On the corner of Budapest's busiest street sat a large wooden chest. A note on top read: "Please use for the funerals of victims of the uprising." The unguarded chest was full of money.

Three 60-ton Russian tanks shook the buildings on a narrow street. Chasing the monstrous enemy were three youths holding rifles in a small open truck. Tanks are powerful, but if someone is willing to risk jumping onto a tank to throw a Molotov cocktail, a tank is vulnerable. One just needs courage, and the young Hungarian freedom fighters had it.

A Soviet tank division was coming across the Danube from Buda to Pest. Teenage schoolgirls held hands in a chain as they stood at the end of the bridge, opposing the tanks. It was like a picture from *Mad Magazine*. The lead tank stopped, the top opened, and a Russian officer appeared.

"What are you doing here?" he demanded.

"What are you doing here?" the girls replied.

"We came to fight the fascists!" the Russian declared.

"No, you came to fight against us," the girls answered.

"Who are you fighting against?" asked the Russian.

"Against the secret police." The Russians joined them and fought on the side of the revolution.

We heard on the radio that the West had donated a considerable supply of medicine and that it was available at the Austrian border. I proposed that we go to fetch some of the medicine. Our caravan consisted of four personal cars, two in front and two at the end, with four trucks between, each marked with a red cross. Before we left, I asked the head surgery nurse what she wanted from Austria. She asked for an orange—something we hadn't seen in decades.

On the way to the border we stopped at an oil refinery to fill our gas tanks in the name of the revolution, which meant we didn't have to pay for it. Meanwhile cars full of Western ambassadors and their families were fleeing the country. Huge flags showing their national identifications floated over their cars.

I stopped and asked them where they were headed. "To Austria" they said. I wished them *auf wiedersehen.* We eventually caught up with them, and when we did I gave a signal, and we cut the middle of their convoy. They honked their horns in protest, but we held our ground and enjoyed their protection to the border. The Russians recognized their diplomatic status and let them go through, even with the strange cars mixed between.

At the border were many refugees and much confusion. The Austrians let us drive in because we said that we wanted to pick up donations from the West. To be in Austria, in freedom, was a huge dream. In Communist

Hungary, in those days, anyone who bought a ticket for a train going in a westerly direction (toward the border) had to provide an acceptable explanation for the trip or risk years of imprisonment. So instead of slowing down at the border, we drove full speed toward Vienna.

At the next village, the Austrian military was waiting for us; it had blocked the highway and we had to stop. While the soldiers surrounded those of us in the first car, the other cars sped past. When the soldiers turned around in surprise, we pulled around them and followed our compatriots at full speed. We caught up with them and together reached the outskirts of Vienna, where we found the chief of police, waiting for us with an escort.

The chief told us, "You can have political asylum, but you cannot use Hungarian government cars in Austria without permission." I told him we did not want political asylum, but we wanted to see Vienna. The police chief offered a little Volkswagen bus that could accommodate eight persons, but there were 16 of us.

"No room for more than eight," he said.

We said we were sorry, but for us it was all or none.

So we didn't see Vienna. We went back to pick up our supplies and returned to Budapest.

Along the way an Austrian man offered to come with us to fight against the Russians. I advised him to stay home because—even with his help—it was unlikely we would win. (A few weeks later, he probably was grateful for my advice.) He gave me a bottle of cognac; I needed it. I became completely drunk and vomited across the border, fully aware of the hopelessness and stupidity of our return. I was intoxicated not only by the cognac but also by the spirit of the idealistic revolution, regardless of the consequences.

When I returned to the hospital, I gave the head nurse an orange.

"You see, I am a fool," I said. "If I had not kept my promise, I would be free now. Here is your damned orange!"

I went to see the injured patients and gave them all— even the Russians—oranges and candies. "These are from our Western friends," I said.

For ten days it appeared that the revolution had succeeded. The new government declared Hungary to be independent and neutral. I did not have any illusions about the outcome of the revolution. I was surprised to hear that the Russians who had been brought in to assist the Communists in stifling the revolution were leaving the country. In fact, they did not leave; they only withdrew from Budapest to make it appear they were gone.

Idealism did not last long. Criminals emerged. Western outcries did not amount to much, and President Eisenhower reassured Khrushchev he had no intention of interfering. I do not think Khrushchev needed much encouragement. Heavy cannons surrounded Budapest, and airplanes bombarded the city and the rebels. The world was standing by. The United Nations held a meeting.

I had lost 18 pounds and was exhausted and defeated. I faced another danger. People accused of bringing weapons instead of food and drugs from Austria were being tortured and executed. My job was in jeopardy if I did not go back to the hospital for premature babies. I asked a doctor friend to send me to a sanitarium to recuperate. I chose one of those near the Austrian border, and on the second day I walked across the border into Austria.

A few weeks later the police were looking for me. Some of those with whom I worked in the hospital during the revolution were executed; most were jailed for years. The

Communists did not allow the practice of religion. But according to a Russian superstition, burying someone face down means he or she will go to hell, and they put all their executed victims in common unmarked graves, face down.

I was one of 200,000 Hungarians who took refuge in the West in the last months of 1956. Many thousands had died in the fighting. All of the Communist Parties in Western Europe disengaged themselves from the centralized influence of the Communist Soviets, and people on both sides of the Iron Curtain realized that the invulnerability of the Soviet Union was a myth. The Hungarian Revolution opened the door for East German, Czech, and Polish uprisings. It was the first break in the iron grasp of the Communist system, which disintegrated three decades later.

Thirty-seven years later, in 1993, I received a letter from the Hungarian embassy in Washington, D.C., saying I had received a medal from President Göncz Árpúd of Hungary for heroic action in the liberation of Hungary during the 1956 revolution. I must admit that receiving a medal is preferable to hanging. (I still wonder about those rewarded in 1957 for putting down the revolution.)

But the real heroes are those who gave their lives, and their reward was a few days of freedom before they died.

American Years

(1957–)

The Journey to America

December 21, 1956. A U.S. Navy transportation boat, the *General Eltinger*, was in the harbor of Bremehaven, Germany, ready to sail with 1,764 Hungarians aboard. On the shore, German prostitutes were waving and crying.

"Why are they crying?" I wondered. Maybe it was because they were losing potential customers.

I heard myself paged over the ship's loudspeaker. The page was from a rabbi from Buffalo, New York, who greeted me and said, "I've ordered kosher food for a hundred people. Will that be enough?"

"I think so," I replied. "I am the only Jew on board!"

Two days later the boat left and sailed into the biggest Atlantic storm of the 20th century. Within a few days, only eight of us were showing up for meals in the dining area; the rest were sick. I was so thrilled to be going to America that I even learned to love ketchup!

At dawn on January 1, 1957, we arrived in New York harbor. What a feeling! I know that some people have criticized Columbus for opening America to foreign settlers. But the millions of us who have suffered suppression, prosecution, and the lack of opportunity over the past few centuries—and those who will suffer the same in the future—are grateful to Columbus.

Before I disembarked, a medical admiral asked whether he could do something for me. I gave him my brother Paul's telephone number in New York and asked the admiral to let him know of my arrival. When he phoned Paul and introduced himself as Admiral such-and-such, Paul thought he was the object of a New Year's Day joke.

"And this is General Fisch," he replied before hanging up.

January 1, 1957, was not only the beginning of a new year. For me it was also the beginning of a new life.

Forensic Medicine

In my last year at the Semmelweis Medical School in Budapest, I studied forensic medicine. It was so fascinating to me that I often ate my sandwich with gusto during the autopsies—to the amazement and disapproval of my classmates.

The most important lesson I learned is that in any criminal situation there are two possible causes. The most likely is the logical consequence of cause and effect. The other involves randomness and accident. The majority of criminal cases are easily solved if the motive is known and the perpetrator can be found. The random crime is much harder to solve unless the criminal leaves evidence, is witnessed, or acts in a pattern.

When I arrived in New York City in 1957, I went to live with my brother Paul in his efficiency apartment in Greenwich Village. I got a job as an intern in a New Jersey hospital.

At the time, Paul was seeing an attractive young woman. One day he started to receive strange phone calls from a man who refused to identify himself. At the beginning the calls were short, and they occurred in the early evening. As time went on, they came late at night and in the early morning, and their tone grew vulgar and threatening. The police weren't able or even interested in getting involved. The phone company tried to help, but the calls were too short to be traced.

The situation became more complicated when the phone calls followed my brother to restaurants. To foil the caller, he changed his pattern of getting around the city and stopped making restaurant reservations in advance. He eventually hired a detective. But all these efforts were in vain. The phone calls followed him whenever he dined out.

Because the phone calls to the apartment disturbed my precious sleep, I decided to apply my forensic skills to the situation. I understood that it is complicated to follow someone in New York City, especially someone who changes his patterns and modes of transportation. Therefore I concluded that someone at the restaurants was tipping off the caller. I told my brother to keep an eye on his date—was there a relationship between the phone calls and her visits to the powder room?

There was. It turned out she was in love with a married man and wanted to make him jealous by letting him know she was seeing another man. My brother was furious, and after blowing up at her, he never received another threatening nuisance call.

And I slept much better.

Minneapolis

Just about everything in my life has been an accident. I think even my birth was unplanned.

When I arrived in the United States, I was fortunate to meet some outstanding physicians. One was Margaret

Smith, a specialist in pediatric infectious diseases at Bellevue Hospital in New York. After a one-year internship at a hospital I hated, I asked her to help me find a good place to further my education. I didn't have the faintest idea where to go. She showed me a map of the United States and marked certain places with one, two, or three stars, based on their ranking as medical teaching institutions.

For no particular reason I pointed to a three-star location in Minnesota. She told me that the University of Minnesota Hospital had one of the top pediatrics departments in the country, and she gave me the name of the person responsible for the training program there.

I arrived in Minneapolis on June 27, 1958. I had mixed feelings—a combination of fear and excitement about coming to a completely unknown place where I didn't know a single person. I had a chance—an unlimited opportunity to begin a new life, and for the first time my future depended entirely on me. The subsequent half-century has given me more than I dreamt possible: profession, friends, art, music, joy, my beautiful daughter, and my wonderful wife. Who could ask for anything more?

Pain

During my pediatric internship at the University of Minnesota Hospital, the general belief among doctors was that newborns could not feel pain. That was hard for me to swallow.

One day I received an infant for a diagnostic workup. He was about four months old, and he had a tumor behind his pharynx. I noted that he frequently hit himself on his forehead and cried. Clearly he was in pain.

Some years later I wanted to test the concept that newborn infants are insensitive to pain. I met Megan R. Gunnar of the University of Minnesota's Child Development Institute, who would become a well-known expert on pain in young children. We studied the cortisol readings of baby boys before and after circumcision to measure their stress levels. We found that their cortisol levels increased tenfold following the procedure (just as for adults going through surgery without anesthesia) and took two hours to return too normal. Of course, these infants responded to pain!

Following the procedure, babies immediately picked up by their mothers stopped crying, despite the pain. Why? Because they felt the comfort of their mothers' touch and closeness, and at the same time they wanted to reward their mothers for picking them up. That's pretty good communication for someone a few days old!

Phenylketonuria

In 1933 a Norwegian doctor, Asbjørn Folling, saw two mentally disabled siblings whose urine had a peculiar odor. Folling identified abnormal chemicals in their urine and the disease he called phenylketonuria (PKU). This was a breakthrough; no one had previously discovered a metabolic cause of mental disability.

Approximately 5 to 10 percent of the total protein a person consumes is an essential amino acid called phenylalanine. People with PKU, an inherited metabolic disease, lack an enzyme in their livers that allows their bodies to break down this amino acid. In the past, persons with this defect became severely mentally disabled.

Many years after Folling's discovery, a German doctor,

Horst Bickel, began prescribing a special diet for PKU patients who were already retarded, and they showed some minimal improvement.

In the 1960s, a pediatrician at the University of Minnesota was treating families with PKU children, some with more than one profoundly disabled child. Before leaving Minnesota, he asked me to follow these patients. Doing so was hard for me emotionally. After we learned about the diet being used for such patients in Germany, we prescribed the diet for a beautiful 17-month-old child with blue eyes and blond hair. When his mother put him down, he was like a limp rag; he was unable to sit, and, of course, he could not talk. Two weeks after he started the diet, he was able to walk, and he began to speak. It was indeed a medical miracle!

Next I made a number of home visits to see whether any of the mothers of a PKU child with PKU had delivered another. I took blood from the newborns for early diagnosis. For the new PKU babies we began the diet soon afterwards, so that no mental damage would occur.

Then a 13-month-old girl named Margaret came to our PKU clinic. Unfortunately for her, it was too late for the diet to reverse the damage. When her uncle, Dr. Robert Guthrie, learned that she had PKU, he developed a simple method for detecting the disease at birth. The Guthrie Test is now used for newborn infants all over the world.

With more than 30 years of effort, difficulty, anxiety, love, and compassion, the PKU Clinic at the University of Minnesota has become internationally known. The clinic has treated hundreds of families. More than half my PKU patients have graduated from high school and gone on to college. This is the result not only of medical research and treatment but also of the power of loving, caring parents dedicated to making their children's lives better. Their commitment and determination have brought gradual improvements, a steady progress that should never stop.

In 1995, I received an honorary doctorate from the Hungarian Pediatric Association for my work with PKU. But my greatest reward has been in seeing hundreds of magnificent children overcome PKU and grow into laughing, playing, working, loving, receiving, and giving people. On June 2004, I coauthored a paper on how a woman with PKU could have a healthy baby without any dietary restriction by using a gestational carrier to prevent the transmission of abnormalities.

My blood relatives died in concentration camps because of hatred. Medicine and love have given me an extended family, its members numbering in the hundreds.

Twins

Twins are fascinating. After hearing many lectures and stories about them, I finally had two identical twin baby boys referred to my clinic. PKU patients require close dietary supervision to restrict their protein intake. Because infants grow rapidly during the first year of life, we saw PKU patients every two weeks in their first two months, every month or two for their first year, and frequently thereafter. Thus, I had plenty of opportunity to observe my patients over the years.

One of the twins was a little taller and heavier than the other at birth, but their development was synchronized. If one's growth sped up or slowed down, so did that of the other. If one's blood protein levels increased or declined since the previous visit, so did the other's. One began walking in the morning, the other that same afternoon.

Then I witnessed an amazing incident. Whenever the boys had a blood test, each one received two lollipops. They both liked the color red, and that is what they always requested. One day they entered the lab one at a time. They did not see each other on the way in or out. When the first twin came out, he had only one lollipop, and it was yellow. His mother asked him why he didn't bring a red one, too.

"I forgot, but my brother will bring me one," he replied.

And he did.

Project Read

I started to work in the pediatric clinic at St. Paul's Ramsey Medical Center in 1991. Most of my patients were indigent, and many of their parents were foreign-born refugees. When babies came for their four-month visit, I usually suggested to the mothers that they read to their infants and show them pictures. But the parents seldom understood my suggestion or my intent, which was to introduce children to books at an early age. In fact, many of their homes did not even have books.

Research shows that children whose parents read to them do better in school. But many families are not able to give their young children this advantage. Once children are mobile, they are more easily distracted, and an important teaching opportunity is lost. As a doctor I decided to do something about this. (The word *doctor* comes from the Latin *docere*, "to teach.")

Our clinic's large waiting room did not have a single book or magazine. The only distraction was the television set, which parents and children alike watched attentively.

One day I brought some magazines from home and put them in the waiting room.

"You shouldn't do that," one of the nurses told me. "People will take them home."

It struck me that this was exactly what we needed, and the idea for Project Read was born.

Large, colorful signs on the waiting room wall now greet visitors in English and six other languages with the message "Read to Your Child." The television set is turned off. Volunteers read—in English—to preschool children, using puppets and other attention-getting items related to the content of the books. Early-childhood educators helped us to select the books, and we purchased them with funds from private donors and foundations. Each child receives a book to take home and keep.

The experience has been rewarding for everyone involved: children, volunteers, and parents. As one mother said, "From now on, I will have to read to my children."

The Minnesota Medical Association has endorsed Project Read. The University of Minnesota Hospital and Clinic have since adopted the concept, as has Health Partners, a large health maintenance organization with many clinics. My goal is for every Minnesota clinic to allow volunteers to read to preschool children in their waiting rooms. I tell my fellow physicians that when they discuss a child's nutrition with his or her parents, they should also discuss nutrition for the mind—like reading a book every day.

The beauty of Project Read is its simplicity. It requires only good intent, a little effort, some volunteers, and a small amount of money.

In Tibet the custom in the past was to choose a two-year-old boy from a humble, illiterate family, who then receives an intensive education and at 18 becomes the Dalai Lama. Early reading improves every infant's potential—whether or not he is destined to sit in that high seat.

The Sweet Tooth

During a meal, it is possible to stop eating even when what sits before you is your favorite dish. But if you eat something sweet, like a piece of chocolate after the meal, you often have an urge to eat more. Have you ever wondered why?

I was responsible for the newborn nursery at the University of Minnesota Hospitals for decades. One day an intern showed me an infant who was only a few hours old. He thought the baby, who could not swallow, had esophageal atresia, a congenitally abnormal closure of the tube leading from the pharynx to the stomach, and the baby was not allowed to drink at all.

The infant was well developed, of normal size, and appeared to be hungry. Because of the drinking restriction, we tried to feed the baby saline solution to avoid any harmful effects from aspirating milk. But the baby did not even attempt to suck. An experienced nurse commented that babies don't like salt but that they do like sugar. When we switched to a 10 percent sugar solution, the infant swallowed normally, finishing off the bottle in a great hurry. The newborn had no abnormality.

A few years later I read a study about how newborn babies respond to different concentrations of sugar water. The more concentrated the sugar, the stronger the suction and the heart rate. My brilliant friend Samuel Bessman, professor of pediatric biochemistry, nutrition, and pharmacology at the University of Southern California, has pointed out that in nature, foods that contain sugar and taste sweet (including meat) are rarely poisonous and, therefore, safe to eat.

That's why it's so hard to follow the recommendation to avoid sugar in our diet. It's against our instinct and nature!

Alex

Since the day my daughter Alex was born, I have seen the world differently. Her being seems the reason for my birth. When Alex was four years old, we read fairy tales together. Once I pretended to be the wicked stepmother in Snow White and offered her an imaginary apple.

"Take it, my dear," I said in a distorted witch's voice. "It is very delicious."

"No thank you. I am not hungry," Alex replied in frightened politeness.

Alex was about five years old when we stepped into an elevator at the University Hospital.

Looking at the buttons, she turned to me and asked, "Which channel, Daddy?"

My First Art Show

One of the delights of my new life in the United States was that, after I completed my residency at the University of Minnesota, I was able to study art. I began at the Minneapolis College of Art and Design and continued there and at other venues for ten years, simply for fun. I started with drawing classes, then painted at home with oils, then gouache.

The first showing of my paintings took place in the late 1960s in Worthington. A colleague had arranged the show in this small town in southwestern Minnesota, once called "The Turkey Capital of the World.

I came a day before the exhibit opening and stayed in the only hotel in town, an inn most likely preferred by trophy-winning turkeys. My photograph appeared in the *Worthington News*—right under an article entitled "How to Make Pigs Fatter."

Worthington is a five-hour trip from Minneapolis. Nevertheless, five of my friends came to see the exhibit. Besides those five, only two other people, strangers to me, showed up.

As soon as I started to speak to the seven assembled guests, one of the strangers stood up and asked, "Is this the movie program that was scheduled for today?"

When I said that it wasn't, the two left.

Since then I have had successful shows with larger audiences who stayed longer. But I have never laughed more than I did at that one.

Opening Remarks
at the Weisman Art Museum, Minneapolis

Light from the Yellow Star—
A Lesson of Love from the Holocaust

April 6, 1994

Ladies and Gentlemen: I am honored and deeply moved to have the privilege and opportunity to speak in the name of those who cannot speak anymore.

I would like to avoid the usual acknowledgments and thank-yous—not because I am not grateful and thankful for those who have made this show and book a reality, but because this exhibit differs greatly from most shows, in subject as well as intent.

On the first evening of the Jewish holy day of Passover, the youngest child traditionally asks, "Why is this night different from all other nights?"

I would like to raise a similar question: "Why is this show different from all others?"

It does not require understanding, because what happened there [the Holocaust] is incomprehensible. I cannot describe it, because it cannot be told appropriately or adequately described in words. I cannot explain it, because there cannot be an explanation for it. It cannot be visually comprehended, because no light is contrast enough for its darkness. Then what is my purpose, with my limited abilities and resources? It is an attempt to describe a feeling, a cry in the dark; it might be even a spark of hope in the darkness.

I am not qualified enough as an artist to attempt the impossible task of expressing the magnitude of the human tragedy of the Holocaust—but who is? I honestly feel that the material of this show is not a product of my own abilities. Rather, it came from within me. I was merely a tool, an instrument of its expression.

Fifty years ago, at age 19, I was one of millions faced with imminent death merely for being a Jew in a German concentration camp. But being a participant in the most organized, systematic extermination of any religious group in the history of mankind does not make me either an objective witness or a reliable historian of that time. My presence serves none of those purposes. I am not only unable, but indeed I do not intend, to recall the horrors of those days and the nightmares that followed.

A quotation from Joseph Campbell's introduction to *The Power of Mythology* provides the most appropriate description of my motivation. It reads: "Privation and suffering alone open the mind to all that is hidden to others." What I would like you to remember is not the horror but the beauty created by human virtue and enlightened by the spirit of suffering. Those dark days demonstrated the strength—and not only the dark, but also the lighter side of mankind.

What could those silent, slaughtered millions ask of us now? To hate and to be unforgiving? The very qualities that led to their demise? Not likely. I believe they would want us to have understanding, compassion, and love. That is what I offer tonight and always—with words, works of art, and deeds.

Whatever the reason for your presence here tonight—friendship, compassion, curiosity—we have one thing in common: we cherish human dignity, and we understand that if we do not stand up against oppression, we become either the victim. or we become the oppressor.

One of the quotations you will see in this exhibit is "I cried out against the brutality but no one listened." Your presence here shows that some do listen. The message I send is, "Remain human—even in inhuman circumstances."

Thank you for being here.

Lake Lucerne

On June 10, 1965, I became an American citizen and immediately applied for a passport. When I received it, I jumped around and kissed it many times in delight. This key opened the door to the world for me. I was the same person as before, but with the passport I could go almost anywhere. I was free! For six weeks I traveled to many places in Europe—Paris, Rome, England, Switzerland . . .

I did not intend to go back to Communist Hungary even though I dearly wanted to see Anna, my dear angel nurse, who was with me from infancy until I escaped after the Hungarian Revolution when I was 32. She taught me by example to cherish patience and love.

Instead of going back, I traveled to Switzerland and stayed in a beautiful old hotel on Lake Lucerne. One day I took a gondola ride up into the mountains. The air changed from the warmth of the lake to the cool breath of the mountain. Going through the clouds, I suddenly saw the gorgeous sight of Mount Pilatus. In the distance I could see the Alps, covered by the mixture of snow and veil clouds under the blue sky.

I stood there as long as I could. The beauty mesmerized me. My descent was via a cogwheel railway; then a boat returned me to the hotel. On the boat I cried from happiness. I liked the idea that my tears became part of the lake and that a little of me would remain forever in this majestic place. But I could not be truly happy without the person who sacrificed so much for me and cared for me for decades. Anna was now crippled, and if I did not see her when I was so close, when would I ever see her again?

Trembling with fear, I realized I had to go back behind the Iron Curtain, certainly, in my mind, to be greeted by guards with submachine guns in their hands, by guards with red stars on their hats, and by vicious dogs. I always hated the Communist system. But I had to see Anna. I would never be able to face myself if I didn't share a little of my happiness with her. So I did go back. My gratitude for all she had given me overcame my terror of returning to that dark world.

The Darkness Within

Depression can be inherited, and stress is often a contributor. I think that was what finally brought down the curtain on my gradually darkening mind.

Astrophysicists describe the slow, swirling effect that precedes the appearance of black holes. That's how I felt. Near a black hole, time becomes irrelevant; there is neither past nor future. I lived in a timeless bubble, completely lacking a present. I said, "I was" instead of "I am." Simple motion was extremely difficult, as was mental activity; no feeling remained. Mere existence was so overwhelming a burden that nothing was more desirable than to end it. Fortunately, I failed to carry even that to completion.

My friends, my colleagues, and my work with children and their families brought me back to this world. I returned from hell for a second time. My first liberation—from a Nazi death camp—required nations and armies, years of preparation, and millions of sacrificed lives. My second liberation was fought inside—cell by cell, minute by minute, hour by hour, for weeks and months. I was alone with my fears, doubts, and nightmares. Life appeared to be futile, but I learned a great deal from it. The patient informed the doctor.

We pronounce, and we believe, that we live in the "modern age." But in the field of mental illness we are barely out of the Dark Ages. Research and treatment are much more widely available for drug addicts and alcoholics than for the mentally ill. Although 18 percent of the people in the United States suffer depression and fewer than 1 percent have HIV/AIDS, the National Institutes of Health spent an estimated $16 per person for research on depression and $2,293 per person for research on HIV/AIDS in 2005.

Many people still consider mental disease to be nothing more than a character weakness. The mentally ill are often a source of embarrassment and shame to their families. For example, I was not allowed to see my daughter's friends when they came to the house. Whereas once the yellow star had marked me, now I was marked by the dark stigma of mental illness. I am unable to decide which was more disgraceful. In the first instance, I knew that nothing was wrong with me; the torment was from outside. In the second, the torment was within; something was wrong with me!

Thanks to Prozac and support from a dedicated colleague, I recovered, but the price was considerable. Shock therapy made me forget some of the past, and the medication gradually took away my enjoyment of sex. My temporary and involuntary celibacy enabled me to concentrate on some things I otherwise could not have done. Still, the desire for deep love remained, and I longed for someone to fulfill it. As the American army, which liberated me, gave me back my life, so my new wife, Karen, gave me back the joy of life and love.

Only after being in the dark do we truly appreciate the light. In our final session, my psychologist gave me some of the best advice I have ever received. For a whole hour I had complained about everything imaginable. He listened carefully, then said, "It will be worse."

That cured me for good. At that moment I understood that today is the best—and perhaps the only—day we have, and we must make the most of it.

My First Date as a Divorced Man

Ten years after a traumatic divorce, I still had neither the courage nor the desire to have a personal relationship with a woman. A man cannot be careful enough. Nevertheless, I enrolled in many evening courses so as to have some human contact beyond that in my work.

One of the courses took place in a synagogue; a rabbi taught it. About 25 participants of different ages and backgrounds attended. Lively discussions followed each lecture. I eventually noticed a pleasant-looking woman, not only because of she was attractive but also because her comments and ideas closely paralleled my own.

One night after class, I finally worked up the courage to ask her to join me for dinner at a nearby Jewish delicatessen. She accepted. We had a lively conversation, and after many years I began to feel somewhat alive again. When we finished the meal and were ready to leave, I asked whether I could see her again.

"I'm sorry but I can't," she responded.

When I asked her why, she said, "I'm a nun, and I leave next week for Rome."

Finally I meet someone likable, in a synagogue, and she turns out to be a nun. As I said, a man cannot be careful enough!

Minot Air Force Base

I have visited the U.S. Air Force base in Minot North Dakota three times. The first was when the Cold War had already become lukewarm. The other two were on Holocaust memorial days, when I was invited to speak to the military and their families.

My fascination with aviation began in my childhood, when I saw American B-17s in the sky during World War II and longed to be with them, flying away to freedom. On my first visit to Minot, I was just one of many tourists. The horrible, destructive capability of the rockets in their silos there was beyond comprehension. We also saw the most sophisticated electronic surveillance that protected the base along with ever-present guards to prevent unauthorized entry and fatal accidents. One of the guards trained German shepherds. I asked him what the dogs were used for.

"Oh," he said, "they are the best protection we have."

On succeeding visits, I was allowed to see the B-52s. After five decades the B-52s remain a most versatile and potent weapon. Their size and capacity are enormous. Their fuel tanks hold more than a car would use in 40 years. Their surveillance equipment can detect a car's license plate from a cloudy night sky.

The crew members were as fascinating as their planes. When I asked one enthusiastic pilot why he wanted to work on a B-52, he said: "You cannot imagine the feeling of the power of eight jet engines behind me."

The pilots were surprised when I told them I had

worked for the air force during World War II. They asked me what I did.

"I was a target!" I explained. I will always be grateful that I was. It led to my survival.

Prison

I had been asked to talk to prisoners in the Oak Park Heights Penitentiary in Stillwater, Minnesota. (The idea of prison reminded me of some marriages, hopefully not all life sentences.) Many people, thinking I would not be safe among those who had committed violent crime, advised me not to go to the prison, but I was curious and I accepted. I had not have the vaguest notion of what I would say, but I came to the conclusion that my speech would not be about humanity, love, or respect. The inmates probably received numberless moral lectures, though given where they were, the subject was moot. I decided to tell them about what happened to me and what I was doing with that experience.

Two female guards greeted me when I arrived. After being carefully checked, I passed through steel doors under TV monitors and went through repeated personal checks. Finally I reached the lecture room. To reassure me, the two guards showed me the gadgets on their belts that could be used to call for help. (I was almost reassured.) A guard told me there were 400 prisoners, each locked in a single cell. Many of them were completely isolated and could not communicate with one another, even during recreation. Some well-behaved prisoners did janitorial work for compensation. If they did not have a high-school diploma, they had to take courses and tests so as to qualify for the work.

No one but I was in the room when I was supposed to begin talking. The guards told me that the inmates had a choice about coming. At the end of the corridor was a metal detector and guards wearing rubber gloves. Gradually the prisoners came into the room. I stood at the door and greeted each of them, shaking his hand. (I had been thoroughly checked for contraband.)

I thanked the inmates for coming and said I was looking forward to talking to them. I was not afraid; neither did I talk with them differently from how I would talk with anyone else. They were my audience. My assistant (who helped with the projector) had been in complete isolation for 15 years. Approximately 27 were in the room. Among them, three or four seemed to be "out of it." I thought they were mentally slow. The rest behaved and listened as attentively as any other interested adult audience. At the end of my talk, they applauded and asked questions. One of the guards told me that the inmates had never responded so well to a speaker.

When I was leaving, a huge black man came to me and said, "How did you do it? How did you stop hating?"

I told him it was not easy, but I could not live any differently. He said he was filled with hatred and could not get over it. He thanked me and said that he learned from me and was grateful for my talk.

Watching him walk away, I understood him well; he felt the way I felt when I left the concentration camp.

Roman Swindlers

One thing I've learned during my travels is to protect my valuables. I carry $20 in small currency in the right pocket of my trousers. I keep a larger amount in my left pocket under tissues and a credit card in my shirt pocket. My wallet is in my back pocket, but it is empty.

In Rome, I made a point to visit Bernini's *The Ecstasy of St. Theresa* in the Church of Santa Maria Della Victoria. According my guidebook, "Marble has never been made to look so supple or to express so accurately the texture of the rough cloth of the Carmelite habit, of light veiling and the delicacy of human flesh." I left the church enchanted by the heavenliness of that spiritual sculpture. Like a typical tourist in the Eternal City, I carried a map in my hand and had my camera around my neck. No one would mistake me for an Italian.

A small car stopped, pulled up next to me, and a middle-aged man rolled down the window and asked me in Italian-accented English whether I could help him. He said he was lost (that made two of us) and asked for directions. I was trying to show him our location on my map; he opened the car door and invited me to get in. I did so but kept the door open. He told me he lived in France and was just visiting.

With Italian charm, he thanked me profoundly. "You are so nice to me that I have to give you a gift," he said. He reached into back seat and handed me a brand-new, cellophane-packed, imitation-leather sports jacket. I really didn't want it, but I enjoyed the show and thanked him repeatedly.

He asked me where I was from, and when I said I was from Minneapolis, he said his mother had visited there. I commented on the coincidence and expressed regret at missing the opportunity to meet his mother. Then he asked about my family. When I told him I had a daughter, he reached back again and gave me another jacket as a gift to her. I then saw that he had quite a supply of jack-

ets. He continued to thank me for my kindness to him—
and then we came to the real reason for our meeting.

He told me to look at the car dashboard. All the instruments were gone. "Last night," he said, "They broke into
my car, stole the instruments and took my credit cards
as well."

How odd, I thought. that the thieves left behind all
those jackets. I asked how could I help him. He said he
needed money for gasoline.

"Okay," I said, "let's go to a gas station."

But he didn't want me waste my valuable time. He just
wanted money. With pleasure, I took $20 in Italian cur-
rency out of my pocket and gave it to him.

"That is not enough," he said. "How about dollars?
How about credit cards?" I told him that was all I had
and got of the car. With a sour face, he drove away.

I stood with the two jackets I had just acquired for
$20. They were worth $160. What they say is true: when
you travel, look out for swindlers.

Musings about Human Nature
and Society

The Conflict between Body and Mind

A fascinating fact of astronomy is that when we look at the stars we see them as they were light years (millions and billions of years) ago.

Similar things are happening here on earth without our awareness. For example, the human body is ancient (I am not talking about myself at 80-plus years). According to geneticists, it takes a million years to achieve only a half-percent change in basic genetic makeup. We have bodies created for another time and lifestyle, and most of our conflicts can be explained by the difference between our bodies and our more quickly changing cerebral-cortex tissue.

In an era of rapid change, the distance between the body and its environment increases, creating more difficulties in adaptation. The most obvious conflict between mind and body is the consumption of food. Our stomachs want to eat more while our brains say no.

Physicians and biologists, who use modern technology, are still puzzled by the mystery of creation and human development. If they wish to understand the present, they must trace backwards to that one, single cell.

Rapid changes in medical, biological, and physical science create an increasing distance between our comprehension of new methodologies and their nonmedical implications, especially regarding moral acceptance and law. Two examples are the current debates over privacy in the use of the Internet and the parental rights related to frozen sperm in cases of divorce or death.

According to astrophysicists, the universe is expanding and galaxies are moving away from each other at high speed. This is analogous to the widening gap between our human body and our intellect and environment. For example, we have considerable difficulty in coming to terms with death. With the expanding body of information on DNA, genetics, and disease, we are discovering more hereditary conditions at an early age and predicting when severe physical, mental, and neurological deterioration and even death, will occur. How do we cope and live with such information?

We were made for an isolated cave existence, yet most of us now live in crowded metropolises. We were made to live according to self-rule, in which our needs require instant satisfaction. Now we submit to rules and regulations that may protect us but do little to satisfy our desires. In the wilderness we followed no principles; strength was the only dominating force. Now we have the illusion that something other than strength plays a more influential role in our everyday life.

The most significant conflict is between the demands of the body and the required modifications in the brain. A loving, protecting, safe, and stimulating parental environment enriches the development of an infant or a child. It begins at an early age with friendly, secure surroundings, melodic sounds and smiling faces, followed at a later age by exposure to the harshness of the outside world. When we were fed and supplied with safe foods, there was no need to be cautious until we explored the unknown and learned that some food might be spoiled or even deadly. Life in duration as well as opportunity was limited. We learned to trust our own kind and to distrust others.

But now the boundaries have changed, the differences are de-emphasized, and there is no clear distinction between friends and adversaries. In addition, within any group, some follow the accepted rules while others ignore them.

Time has quickly changed the outside world, but inside we have changed very little. This conflict is the fundamental reason for most of the difficulties we face within ourselves and with others.

We want to eat as much as possible, more than we actually need, and we try to save energy by reducing unnecessary activity. Our basic makeup is incompatible with the advice to minimize caloric intake, select healthful nutrients such as fiber, avoid dangerous ones such as cholesterol, and burn excess calories by exercise. This contradiction between what we want and what we know is a constant companion in our daily experience regarding food.

We have to make a living. Our mind accepts this and forces the body to work. But the body wants to save energy. Most people experience boredom, laziness, and even aversion while at work—a conflict between bodily desires and an environmentally necessitated existence.

We emphasize the importance of individuality, yet there is ample evidence that many people prefer to be followers than leaders. Most people want guidelines and boundaries. They want someone else to clear the path. And the consequences can be devastating.

Even with emphasis on religious teaching and moral

values, human history continues to produce wars and mass killings. Methods of killing have progressed in sophistication and effectiveness. There is no evidence that people have become more tolerant or less greedy. This is even more surprising when one considers that modern telecommunications technology brings violence graphically into our homes—scenes that at one time would witnesses only by the perpetrators and the victims.

Violence continues because hate and killing are biological instincts. Being civilized is a learned attitude.

What can we do? We need to know where we came from and to realize that changes must take place within us. We have to modify our feelings and relations with others to avoid not just bloodshed but conflict. We must learn and teach that compassion is not a natural phenomenon and that good behavior requires discipline and self-control. We cannot assume that we are born with all the positive qualities necessary for living in a civilized environment. If we understand that we were created for another environment, then we will realize that the key to being civilized is not to conquer others but to control and modify our own biological nature and change our own behavior.

In the first stage of life we function on a biological level. Some of us enter the second stage by learning and practicing compassion and love, and we become human. But this trait is not hereditary; it must be learned!

We must grow up developing our values and understanding the need to defend them. We must realize the difficulty of learning human values rather than blindly following others. We must not only pursue what benefits us but also consider what benefits others. And finally, we must understand that it is almost impossible to keep up with all the changes around us. At the least we must accept that personal modifications and flexibility are essential to live in harmony with others. When an individual's biological desires and needs collide with those of others, it may be necessary to compromise or yield to exist in a new civilized environment.

Why do we celebrate love only one day a year, on Valentine's Day? Why not practice love all year around and rest for one day, instead?

The First Step toward Humanity

Matisse is one of my favorite artists. Years ago at the Museum of Modern Art in New York City, I saw the largest Matisse exhibit ever shown. More than 450 paintings were on display. Right at the beginning I realized that I could not possibly give each painting equal time and attention. So whenever I entered a gallery, I glanced around to select the paintings I would look at closely and ignored the others. I spent more than four hours there.

Later a friend asked me how I made the choices. I had to think. How indeed? Obviously I might prefer the combination of colors, forms, and subjects of one painting to another. But why? Why did I prefer one thing to another without any clear reason?

Think about going to a party where you don't know many of the other guests. You probably would not talk with every person in the room.

We make some selections unconsciously, the choice based on our previous experience and preferences. In a grocery store people do not take the nicely displayed apples from the front and in an orderly fashion; they make selections. Someone could say that the apples are not similar or that some have imperfections. But what about milk cartons? People also pick these up in a different order. There are no visible imperfections in the milk cartoons. But some may assume that certain locations keep the milk colder and fresher than others. Our brains cannot ignore previous imprints; therefore we are never able to be completely objective.

If we do not see identical things in the same way, how can we expect to see different people in identical ways? We know that even two snowflakes are not the same. We also know that two people carrying out the same task will do it differently and with different results. We can't see the same things in the same ways. According to the laws of quantum mechanics, personal observation itself influences and alters the findings. In other words, each of us comes up with different conclusions to the same observed thing.

Unfortunately, differences in education, nationality, race, and religion even further obscure our already distorted viewpoints.

My favorite television program is *Fawlty Towers*, which has been translated into more than 60 languages. In the original English version, the waiter, a man with limited vocabulary and ability, is Spanish. When the program was shown in other countries, the waiter's nationality was been changed to reflect the national attitudes in the places it was aired.

The easiest way to claim superiority is through birthright and titles. Titled people may feel superior to others through their entire lives. According to the Jewish religion, Jews are God's "chosen people." According to Christians, only through Jesus can someone "go to heaven."

When a child begins walking and heads out the door,

the parents say, "No. You are not safe outside. This is your home." We protect our children out of love, not hate. And from there on we send them to schools, churches, synagogues, and clubs to be with our kind and our preferred people. The selection is based on good, not bad, intentions.

Humans are biological animals, like every other species. In nature there is no evidence of fairness and justice. To become human, children must be taught about morals, values, and respect from an early age.

At the very least, we must offer others the same respect that we expect ourselves—not because we are equals but because we must learn to behave better than biological animals before we can be called human beings.

That is the only way to minimize our inability to make fair distinctions about people. Remember, we have preferences and are incapable of being objective. Justice and fairness are human endeavors that don't exist in biology. To learn civilized behavior is the first step to humanity.

Growth and Development

Growth is a natural phenomenon of existence. It is no less mysterious than life itself. In fact life, growth, and development are inseparable. Growth is a form of changing, not only physically but also spiritually and mentally. Like most of us, I am fascinated by how the universe—and life—evolved. Many of us believe that all life, however small, has a God-like particle inside. We are surrounded by the infinite.

It is astounding to comprehend that whatever made that simple first element had the ability to grow exponentially in complexity. How did the basic six quarks—if, indeed, quarks are the smallest and most original form in the universe—evolve? From the moment of the Big Bang, change has continued, the basic elements constantly developing, altering species and organisms.

I think there is in the basic elements a certain Organizing Factor. It is a dormant factor that under favorable circumstances initiates an increasingly complex structure. The Organizing Factor is present in every conceivable element and material, in living and nonliving organisms. Life itself began with nonliving materials.

In recent years we have found that the bacteria invading the body act according to their specific locations or roles, as do ants and bees. On the mucosa, for instance, they become protectors fighting with antibodies. At the top they are the multiplying invaders, in the middle they are the supporters of the other bacteria that invade. Inevitably, internal forces of cooperation exist in the individual particles for larger tasks that cannot be achieved alone.

It seems to me that the miracle is not what something becomes, but what it is at the start. The complexity is nothing more than hypertrophy specialization; the original element has all the abilities and potential. The amoeba has one single cell that contains all the abilities of more complex organisms.

After fertilization by the father's reproductive cell, the maternal reproductive cell, the ovum, results in a completely unique cell that initiates an unprecedented magnitude of growth. All the other cells that develop from this one have the same blueprint for determining the abilities, functions, and potential of the new person. The magnitude of growth cannot be easily comprehended. The ovum is 130 microns in diameter. The fetus grows 3,846 times in length until birth, up to 50 centimeters.

And the growth is not only reduplication but also a differentiation for multiple specifications. So much happens, and everything has to work precisely. In 96 percent of the time the result is a healthy, normal baby. Whenever I see newborns, I marvel at the miracle. Not bad for a beginner! Imagine a newborn baby continuing to grow at the rate of fetal development. At nine months the baby would be the length of 20 football fields. At 18 months its length would be the distance from New York to Los Angeles; at 27 months, 70 times the distance from Earth to the moon; at 36 months, 500 times of the distance from Earth to the sun; and at 18 years, bigger than the width of the known universe.

The weight of a united ovum and sperm increases six billion times from conception to birth. If a newborn continued to gain weight at that rate, by 27 months it would outweigh the earth! Don't even try to guess its weight at 18 years; we have no comparison for it. Parents must prepare a child for an independent life. As a seed needs water, fertile ground, and sunshine, the newborn needs nourishment and a supportive, loving environment.

Think about how much a child must learn from first breath to first word, from year one to year six, from first step to first day of school. Then come 12 years of school and physical, social, intellectual, and sexual maturation. Then, the completion of further education or vocational skills. Whatever the individual abilities determined by inheritance, without emotional and intellectual support from outside, no one can achieve his or her potential.

Our bodies change little over time. Remember, it takes a million years for DNA to change half a percent. The social environment of today demands a different lifestyle for our bodies than it did in the past—but our bodies are not adapting as quickly as the environment is changing. An essential ingredient in development is adaptability, which requires the modification of behavior. This can be difficult, both physiologically and mentally.

We live in a crowded environment, and we must take the needs and desires of others into consideration. We need a different attitude towards each other in this ever more crowded world. We must alter our biologically enforced attitudes with broadly accepted civilized laws and customs.

With a growing world population and limited resources, we humans face inevitable conflict. Given our increasingly destructive capabilities, catastrophic mass extermination may occur. If we have any hope of survival, we must replace biological motives with a more constructive approach. Whole societies must grasp the importance of overcoming the biological, animalistic behavior of taking over by force or killing. Instead, we must learn compassion and understanding. Then we can become an important part of holistic growth and development, and we can contribute positively to the ever-changing world within and around us.

Survival of the Fittest

I understand that ten or so years ago an infectious disease specialist announced victory over the bacteria that cause diseases. His false conclusion was based on the belief that then-available antibiotics would effectively eliminate and cure all bacteria-caused disease.

The statement, of course, was incorrect; and it demonstrated misunderstanding of a basic law of nature.

Bacteria have the same ability to adapt that any other living organisms have. Antibiotics may kill the first bacteria, but gradually they develop resistance and then immunity. The new generation of virulent bacteria causes even more severe symptoms. Scientists went back to survey a Pacific island where a hydrogen bomb had been detonated. The whole area was barren. Still, the island was inhabited by a large number of rats. Not only had they survived, but also there was no evidence of increased malignancy or malformation among them.

In the everlasting fight there are no final victors. (Not event the rats!)

Under the Palm Trees

I was enjoying the warmth and sunshine (of which I am deprived for most of the at-least-six-month Minnesota winters) and the sound of the waves of the Atlantic Ocean. It was late morning in a famous "Old World" hotel near Miami. I was sitting in a large white wicker armchair in the Spanish courtyard. In the center was a water fountain surrounded by palm trees, colorful Spanish tiles, and round white tables with umbrellas. Everyone seemed to be enjoying his or her luxurious breakfast, served by an attractive Cuban waitress. The overall comfort made me forget the harsh reality of the world.

At the next table a South American family finished breakfast. The beautiful dark hair of each of the family members contrasted with the cloudless blue sky. On the table a piece of toast was still untouched.

A small daring sparrow dived over the plate and grasped the whole piece of toast in its beak. It tried to fly away, but the size and weight of the toast were too much, and it dropped to the ground between the tables.

The sparrow took only one bite before a pigeon recognized an unexpected meal and chased the brave little bird away. The pigeon consumed a considerable amount of the toast, and then a flock of sparrows got in on the action. They tried to divert his attention by approaching the bread from different sides. The pigeon had a larger beak and took bigger bites; yet it preferred chasing away the other birds to sharing the bread.

Growing frustrated with the increasing number of sparrows, the pigeon stood on what was left of the bread. From that position he showed his dominating power, but he was unable to eat. When a waiter came, the pigeon flew away. The waiter picked up the bread and threw it into a wastebasket. For him the bread was nothing more than a disturbing blight on the immaculate Spanish tile.

For the little sparrow the toast was an overwhelmingly tempting target, and his hunger overcame his desire for safety. The size of bread was beyond his need and capability, but instead of eating some to satisfy his need, he wanted it all. He tried, without success, to get it back to his nest. His eyes were indeed bigger than his stomach.

The pigeon took over by sheer power and indulged himself without concern for others. There was no room for sharing. When he recognized his vulnerability, he used the food to exhibit his power.

And then the bread was gone. But the scavengers, true to their nature, likely moved to another site, their hunger, eagerness, aggressiveness, weaknesses, and struggles starting all over again.

My illusion of being away from the real world was gone. The real world is everywhere, even in the beautiful, isolated courtyard of an elegant old hotel, under white umbrellas warmed by the sun.

Double Standard = No Standard

I studied Latin for eight years in high school. From the first hour, I was always behind. I brought the wrong textbook to my first class, and somehow I could never catch up.

Many people question the value of studying a "dead" language. I have to say that, in spite of my difficulties, I learned things from Latin that made a permanent mark on me. For example, the lecture on the speech of Menenius Agrippa: At one time an element of the Roman population rebelled against the nobility. Menenius Agrippa, a senator, went to the rebels and gave a speech in which he made an analogy between the body and the society: the different parts of the body were upset that some parts made considerable effort in the gathering of food (feet and hands), and chewing the food (teeth and tongue), but the stomach did not seem to contribute to the process. So the more active parts decided to stop feeding the stomach and stopped eating. The consequence was detrimental to the whole and to each part of the body.

I have become a firm believer that each of us—and each segment of the population—plays a part in the wheel moving us towards the future. We are all made from the same material, but we are formed differently and thus have different abilities and qualities. We are not worth more or less, but we play different roles. Pilots have the most glamorous job on an aircraft carrier, but they cannot function or even exist without the support of many others. Everyone's role is essential to the performance of the aircraft.

We all belong to the human race, and none of us has a superior or inferior role; the roles are all just different. I have personally experienced political and systems (Nazism and Communism), in which parts of society were excluded or destroyed. Both systems generated disastrous consequences, not only for the suppressed groups but eventually for the privileged ones as well. Menenius Agrippa's classic story remains relevant.

Various moral and philosophical teachings in both ancient and recent times urge a more advanced democratic society based on equality. Equality in this context initially meant equal opportunity. This has been misinterpreted to mean that every human being is equal. It should be obvious that, although human beings have the same basic components, no one is exactly like anyone else. There is only a 1 percent difference between the DNA of chimpanzees and that of humans. We all use the same letters of the alphabet, but the genius creates masterpieces while others scrawl vulgarity on the walls of toilet facilities. Everything, everyone, is distinguishable and unique.

Almost all of us have experienced feelings of discrimination and helplessness because of background or origin, or even because of profession. Discrimination can originate from a complex body of differences or may be provoked merely by driving a certain kind of car or wearing a certain kind of clothes. Because I have often been treated as a second-class citizen and even as a persona non grata, I am especially sensitive to this issue. I do not accept that someone with a title automatically deserves preferential treatment in any area except his particular specialty, provided his is indeed better qualified than others.

Discrimination grants preference for some, and denies fairness to others. But an attempt to correct past injustices by preferring a particular group of people to others (though they may be less qualified) is a form of discrimination as well.

The human mind prefers simplicity and usually sees

things in two dimensions. We think that if one side of a coin is heads, the other has to be tails. The opposite of a lie is truth. But in this case nothing could be farther from the truth. One injustice cannot correct another.

The Extremes

We think linearly that extremes are the opposite ends of a measure. When we compare, for example, mentally challenged individuals with geniuses, we think these two are the extremes of mental abilities. But the two extremes actually are closer to each other than they are to the median or average. Human functions in the extreme are considered abnormal, regardless of whether the deviation is advantageous (and rewarded) or disadvantageous (and needing support). The deviations come from a malfunction, from over- or under-production.

The concept that extremes are at the opposite ends of a line is not accurate. We think human development starts at the beginning and follows a straight line to the end. We think about time in the same way. But if we look at the extremes, they resemble two ends of an incomplete circle, closer to each another than to the middle.

Exceptions to the norm are frequently evident in nature. Among 200 million sperm, only one completes its destiny. Likewise in art—how many works of art are created and how few become masterpieces? While everything is an attempt at development, it takes an enormous number of repeated efforts and failures to achieve real movement.

There are thousands of mentally challenged people, millions of average people, and few geniuses. Most of the time people prefer to be in the middle—average, inconspicuous, among the majority— because there they feel safer and more secure. Few prefer their lives to be sensational and in the extreme.

Hugging a Child

One of my most rewarding experiences occurred in giving a talk at a high school. At the end I asked for questions, and a girl stood up and said, "Can I give you a hug?"

When I was growing up, physical touch was an expression of closeness between family members and friends. Following each meal, I thanked my parents and kissed them. My friends and I walked hand in hand or kissed when we got together. Touch was an expression not of sexual desire but of human connection.

Now when I speak in schools, the teachers, unfortunately for everyone forbidden to touch their students, always welcome me. How can anyone express joy for children or congratulate their achievements and success without touch?

My talks last about two hours. In the first hour I talk about my experiences and emphasize the importance of remaining human even in inhumane circumstances, by showing respect, compassion, and even love for each other. In the second hour I answer questions.

Once I asked a member of the Jewish organization that helps schedule my lectures to sit in on my conversation with the students. When we left the class, a young boy ran up to me in the corridor and gave me a hug. My companion said, "You should know that some teachers have objected to your hugging and even kissing some of the children."

We live in an unusual time. Humanity, moral values, and appropriate behavior are restricted subjects in schools, and teachers and students cannot express their feelings with a hug. We see human touch as the basis of lawsuits, and we forget that it is the easiest way to express warm feelings.

Thinking and Communication

I am fascinated by the idea that it is impossible to observe reality without changing it. Quantum physics tells us that physical reality is essentially insubstantial. Although all human brains consist of the same elements and follow the same physiological rules, the way a human perceives, comprehends, concludes, and performs depends upon both genetics and experience. Each of us is a unique, unprecedented experiment of nature.

We are obsessed and influenced by time. We think of beginning and end in linear terms, like a measuring stick. But the universe exists in circular form, and the extremes are closer to each other than to the middle. The human brain does not observe even time—past, present and future—equally or linearly.

When two artists paint the same scene, one emphasizes the flowers, another the debris. The person who caused an accident describes it differently from the person to whom it happened or who witnessed it. Can a scientist's project be truly objective?

The universe has common laws, yet the world I live in is not the same as someone else's world. We are lucky if we can communicate with one another to achieve some mutual understanding.

To practice medicine effectively, physicians must recognize this. They must be expert communicators—good at listening, questioning, and explaining. Knowledge and communication are complementary; both are essential in discussing life and death.

But there are many forms of interference between thinking and communication. A few years ago a survey revealed that parents of children with leukemia comprehended only a fraction of the information they received from a pediatric oncologist. We often hear only what we want to hear; we have selective reception. A mother whose child died of leukemia told me that her daughter's last words were "Mother, don't let me die." But a colleague who was there said the last words were "Mother, let me die."

A television program about parents of autistic children showed the parents holding their children's hands and directing their fingers to type on computer keyboards, apparently believing that the sentences and essays were actually written by the children—even though the children clearly were unable to coordinate their hands with their minds and did not know the alphabet. Such methods have been used to give evidence in court.

Recently I saw two young siblings, a boy of seven and a girl of six. Their mother is a veterinary pathologist at the university; their father, who has a master's degree, is the homemaker. The children's responsiveness and eloquence are astonishing for their age. Their father told me that the family does not have a television; instead the parents and their children talk and read. In other words, they communicate a lot.

No technical advancements could or will ever replace parental love, attention, and education in early life. We have an inherent desire to be known and to be heard. Cave paintings, village drums, smoke signals, writing, and speeches convey messages between people. Charismatic orators and compelling writers are already becoming rare commodities. Let us hope they do not become extinct.

Musings about Life and Spirit

Coincidences and Dreams

Inside each of us are millions of bits of information, but our awareness allows us to be in contact with only a few of them at any given time. What we are conscious of is not even the visible tip of an iceberg; it is an incomprehensiblly tiny manifestation of our underlying, immense unconscious. And beyond the five known senses, others may exist that are as yet unknown.

We are even less aware of what is going on inside ourselves than of what is going on around us. Let me illustrate with a few incidents that are difficult to comprehend, though they have really happened.

In the dead of winter 1944, thousands of death marchers, prisoners of the Nazis, marched from dawn to sunset. Sometimes we marched for five days without food or water. Finally, on the night of April 14, we arrived at the notorious Mauthausen concentration camp. The march's toll was evident in our gaunt faces and skeletal frames.

In the dark among 10,000 prisoners, a man came to me and asked, "Are you from Hungary?"

"Yes," I said.

"Did you know George B., from Budapest?"

"He was a friend of mine. We were born on the same

day and year," I answered. "We were together in a labor camp, and he escaped."

"Thank God!" he responded, even though he knew that most of the escapees had been captured and killed. He was George's father.

～✕

After my liberation in the summer of 1945, I returned home to Budapest. There I found my mother and Anna, who had been my governess since I was an infant. Anna's parents had hidden my mother from the Nazis in their home. I ate from dawn to dusk for weeks. But although my physical condition improved rapidly, my emotional state remained blank—no laughing, no crying.

We didn't know where my father was. He had been taken away with many other Jews, destination unknown. One day a man appeared and said he brought a message from my father: He was alive in Germany and had asked us to send a car to bring him back. My mother rushed home from her shop to tell me the good news.

"Do not do anything," I said. "He did not send any message. The messenger and the message are both false. He would have sent a note, at least." It was not easy to deny us even that remote hope.

Months later my mother went to a new hairdresser. In those days, everyone talked about the war, expressing sorrow for lost ones or searching desperately for information about missing family and friends. After the hairdresser told her story, it was my mother's turn. She showed her my father's picture.

"Oh, that's Uncle Zoli," the hairdresser said. "He was with us in the same camp. He was very much loved because even there he gave his food to others, saying, 'I always have enough.'"

My beloved father, who always gave to others, had
starved to death. He was so greatly respected in the camp
that he was, as mentioned earlier, the only one not thrown
into a common grave. The hairdresser eventually led us to
his grave. We brought back his body, and he was the first
to be buried next to the "Memorial for the Martyrs" in the
Jewish Cemetery of Budapest. As his grave was dug and the
coffin lowered, I felt my childhood was being buried with
him, and I started to cry. Those tears were the first sign that
the concentration camps had not erased all my feelings.

I worked as a general practitioner in the Hungarian mining town of Tatabánya, sent there by the Communist
regime as a kind of deportation for being politically unreliable. It was approximately 70 miles from my home
in Budapest, and I traveled back and forth by train. One
night in a dream, a friend warned me, "Be careful of the
train. You will have an accident."

All the trains were crowded. A few people customarily
crossed the rails to board their train from the other side, to
avoid the climbing and pushing on the crowded platform.
On this day I too ran to the other side. I stood facing the
crowd, awaiting my train, which would arrive from the
right. Suddenly I noticed a look of alarm in the onlookers'
faces. I turned to the left and saw a freight train 20 yards
away coming toward me at full speed on the same rail on
which I stood. I leapt ahead between the two trains—one
behind me coming at full speed, the other in front of me,
gradually slowing. Thus I avoided a fatal accident—the
prediction in my dream had come true.

In 1973, my 83-year-old mother asked me to accompany
her to Senta in northern Yugoslavia, where she was born

and raised. Before World War I, the region belonged to Hungary. She wanted to pay homage to her parents and ancestors in the cemetery where their bodies had been buried. We were frustrated in our attempt to locate our relatives in the unattended cemetery. Not a single descendent of the original community had remained. We could not locate her parents' graves. Erosion, lack of care, and overgrown vegetation had erased the names from the headstones. I left a bit of money for the so-called caretaker and asked him to send me the location of my grandparents' graves. I never heard from him.

On the way home, we waited in a junction city at the border for the train from Belgrade to Budapest. Horsedrawn buggies and charming buildings surrounded the square in front of the railroad station, so I took some photos. The next minute a hand tapped me on the shoulder, and a man ordered me to follow him to the police station. I was being arrested for taking a picture of the railroad station.

I raised several objections: First, I did not take a picture of the station; further, the station was been built in the last century, and many pictures of it no doubt already existed; satellites could take better pictures than I; and finally, my mother was 80 years old. and our train would arrive within minutes.

I soon realized that common sense and logic would not prevail. When I argued that I was taking the picture toward the square with my back to the station, the police offered to develop the film—by sending it to Belgrade.

Eventually the police let me go, but they confiscated the film. Fortunately, our train was late (perhaps the time required for investigating spies is built into the train schedule). I decided never again to enter a country where the minds are more primitive than the facilities.

So I thought I had buried Yugoslavia and that cemetery forever. Nevertheless, 22 years later, in 1995, I was giving a lecture at the university in Szeged, Hungary, not far from of the Yugoslavian border. I visited the home of the professor who had invited me to give the lecture, and as she went to the kitchen to fix me a drink, I noticed a newspaper on the living room table. It lay open to an article about a photo exhibit—*The Neglected Jewish Cemetery of Senta*—that had opened that day in an art gallery. Unexpectedly I saw again the forgotten, unmarked graves of my ancestors. The past had returned.

~

In 1967 I took an unforgettable boat trip around the Greek Isles. Each passenger was assigned to particular table for every meal. My table included an amiable couple. The man was a wine connoisseur. At the end of the trip we exchanged cards in case we ever visited the other's hometown. They lived in the Hancock Building in Chicago.

Many years later I went to Chicago to visit a childhood friend, whom I had not seen in the 30 years since we escaped from Hungary. He had become a pathologist. Walking down Michigan Avenue on a sunny Saturday, we passed a fascinating building. My friend said it was the Hancock Building. I remembered the names of my traveling companions, and I went inside to see whether they were in. The man was home and graciously invited me up. I introduced my doctor friend and apologized for our unscheduled intrusion. He was understanding and asked my friend which hospital he worked in. When my friend told him, he said, "Two weeks ago they did a lung biopsy on me in your hospital, and the diagnosis was cancer."

"Yes, I remember," said my friend. "I made the diagnosis."

When we left, my chance acquaintance gave my friend a rare bottle of wine.

One night in a dream, I asked God, "Are we Jews the chosen people?"

God answered, "The world turns on its axis and each segment receives an equal share of sunshine."

In another dream, I was supposed to meet with God. I was in a huge, endless, warehouse-like building. God was late. Suddenly I felt as I never had before. Both space and time vanished. I realized I was experiencing a fraction of His presence, which was the *only* thing there. In His powerful presence, nothing else exists.

Dreams

I read and hear so much about dreams. The current theory is that dreams are made of the random appearance of the billions of pictorial impressions in our brain.

I dream almost every night and often more than once a night. They are more nightmares than dreams. So if I were to tell someone that she was my dream, it would by no means be a compliment. In most of my dreams I am unable to escape. Escaping from the past seems to be impossible as well.

I am not necessarily "out" while I sleep, and I am often aware that I am dreaming. At times, solutions to problems or uncompleted tasks occur to me. Occasionally I wake myself and write down solutions, thoughts, and even designs.

My most amazing dreams are about beautiful, complex woodcarvings, carpets, paintings, and scenery—all in great detail. I can see the details of a carved eagle perfectly from different angles, as if it were real. With a carpet, I can see the complexity of the colored thread. I have even touched them and felt the texture of the material.

But my favorite dream is one of my composing music and humming it to myself. Music to me is the highest human artistic achievement. If there is one thing I regret in my life, it is that I did not pursue my musical education.

Therefore I have difficulty accepting that dreams are strictly the result of random images of past impressions. It seems to me they must partly be an active result of our minds and thoughts, a creative process of our brain.

Ice Sculptures

Every December the people of the city of St. Paul celebrate the "Winter Carnival." One part of the program is a display of beautiful ice sculptures. One winter I went on the first day to see the glimmering beauties. It was unusually warm by Minnesota standards, and the lovely angels, swans, and other figures started to melt. It looked like their tears were dripping to the ground. I was surprised that artists would choose a short-lived material like ice for their creations. Why not marble?

Then I realized that no material lasts forever. Some just last a little longer. For the artist the essence is creation, not duration.

The Value of Time

An observer from another world would see an obvious pattern of existence and activity among earthlings. Most of us are born in a hospital and buried in a cemetery. Between these two points is a confusing zigzag of running back and forth and around—some faster, some slower, some farther, some closer—but from a larger point of view it's only a flicker of time. The only stable points are the beginnings and the ends, though medical advancements have at least doubled life expectancy in the past hundred years.

Our lives are like rubber bands. No matter how much we pull on them, we just stretch the same whole. In the past, people's lives were much shorter. Children went to work at an early age. Now people live longer, but they spend more years being educated, they work longer, they retire later, and they may spend years in a home for the elderly before death. The duration of their lives may be longer, but the essence of their lives is the same.

We think of life as a line with a beginning and end, birth and death, but this concept is a distortion. The finite cannot measure the infinite; the linear concept makes no sense.

We divide and speak of time as divided by equal durations, (years, months, weeks, days, hours, minutes, and seconds). But our own brains perceive time in a different way—past decades seem shorter than decades to come. We know that the speed of light changes according to influence of the gravity of approaching or departing celestial objects. Is time real or like light in Einstein's theory of relativity? Is time real or an illusion?

High-energy physics experiments have shown that protons collide with neutrons and with one another, at nearly the speed of light. Some particles exist for only a fraction of a millisecond, yet during their brief life span they cover distances hundreds of thousands of times their size.

Some insects are born in the morning, mate at noon, and die in the evening. Mosquitoes live three months, and some turtles live for a hundred years. But time makes no difference in the natural laws that govern them: they are born, grow, and reach maturity, age, and die. The duration is an illusion, a product of point of view.

The point of human existence is not how long we live but what we do with this precious gift we call life, or as I prefer to call it, awareness. Everything and everyone is subject to the limits of time. Knowing this distinguishes humans from mosquitoes and protons.

Colorful Frogs vs. Cars

The South American forest frog's brilliant colors are a clear sign of danger, a visual warning of dreadful consequences should one approach—go away, leave me alone!

The drivers of the luminous red, yellow, green Ferrari, Maserati, and Lotus cars on Rodeo Drive in Los Angeles seek another response, their cars extending an invitation—come in.

Looking at Art

When you look around a museum, you can see many visitors walking from one painting to the next, first looking for the label with the name of the painter and the title of the painting. If the painter is famous (Rembrandt, for example), the visitor will sigh and step back, spending more time there than with a lesser-known artist's work.

To a certain extent that response is understandable. After all we live in a world that celebrates fame and the limelight. Every morning large crowds in New York City wait for hours in rain or snow, wearing funny outfits and carrying posters or infants on their arms, waving at the cameras on morning TV news shows.

Once I was at the Boston Art Museum in a gallery of impressionist paintings. One was by Renoir, and it portrayed a young couple. A noisy group of 10-year-olds came in with their teacher. She asked the children which paintings they liked best. Most of them pointed to the Renoir. Then she asked which character they thought was the most important part of the picture. Without hesitation they screamed, "The girl!"

"Why do you think that?" the teacher asked.

"Because she has a red hat on her head," was their answer. They were observant.

Then the teacher told the students that when each of them went into a room in a gallery or museum, they should look around to find the picture they liked most. Only then should they look at the artist and the title.

When I was a young, I met an artist who had just come back from Paris. I asked him how he knew when a painting was good.

He thought for a while and answered, "It hits you in your chest."

So don't look first for the name of the artist—look for what you like, look for a red hat, look for what hits you in the chest!

The Art of Medicine

The relationship between art and medicine has been the subject of considerable discussion. There are strong forces among physicians and others who consider medicine only a science, not an art. For example, they would eliminate the word "art," from "medical arts buildings." Here are my musings on this subject.

Early one morning I was driving on a highway. The sunrise made the sky azure blue, and the full moon shone like a silver seal over the horizon. The moon was large, beautiful, and mysterious. I looked away to pay attention to the traffic. A few seconds later I looked up again, and the moon was gone. What happened? Had the road turned in another direction? Did the moon just fade away? Was it only my imagination? It was none of these. A little industrial smoke had obscured the sight on that glorious morning.

A little smoke can interfere with the view of a celestial object. We perceive only a fraction of a percent of the visible electromagnetic spectrum. Not only are the senses limited, but thoughts can be obscured as well. Miniscule, insignificant factors can influence the mind to the extent that it sees, misinterprets, and miscomprehends light, objects, and. Yet, despite the limited perception of the senses, the human mind appears to have an unlimited ability, reinforced by imagination, to discover, create, and enrich the quality of life.

Imagination can overcome anything. With unlimited imagination, people have been able to invent that which extends beyond the limits of the horizon for human perception, beyond the recognizable, to gather, analyze, comprehend, and create. These human abilities are equally applicable to the fields of art and medicine.

What is art? In my youth, a shoemaker made beautiful shoes for my family. Although it was a long time ago, I vividly remember how the new pairs of shoes shone like mirrors. Just as the shoemaker appeared ready to hand them over, he took them back and rubbed them again and again. He clung to his shoes as a child clings to its mother. He had put his talent, skill, and heart into those shoes; he did not want to give up his most recent "masterpiece."

Regardless of who we are or what we do, we have the choice of being artists—like the shoemaker—or charlatans, in everything we do. When Pablo Picasso was asked, "What is art?" he answered, "What isn't?"

For me, art, in the narrower sense of drawing and painting, is a useful complement to medicine. Not only does it give me as a doctor an opportunity to do something different, but it is also a helpful, supportive addition to my work. Art gives me an appreciation for beauty, color and for life itself. The medical field is a constant battleground where fights with diseases are won and the horizon expands beyond conquered ground. Yet as we face imminent death, the ultimate war is lost. There is no final victory in medicine. We doctors only transform one problem into another so as to prolong life.

With art, however, the product does not deteriorate. While art is an expression of joy for being alive, it is also a response to the fear of death. Art is a victory over mortality. It survives even as the body fades away. Like the ancient peoples who made drawings on cave walls, we want our art to be an immortal monument beyond the mortal body. We want to leave behind a reminder that we were here!

Art provides me a dimension that I do not get in medicine, and that is the lonely experience of creation. Both art and medicine provide opportunity for creativity, but medicine requires the participation of doctor and patient in a cooperative, one-to-one partnership. For an artist, the empty canvas or paper is as exciting as a new patient is for a doctor. Both fields require insight, intelligence, experience, and intuition. But the artist, unlike the doctor, does not need a partner.

Vassily Kandinsky, the first abstract painter, wrote in his book *Concerning the Spiritual in Art*: "If the science of the day before yesterday is rejected by the people of yesterday, and that of yesterday by us of today, is it not possible that what we call science today will be rejected by the people of tomorrow?" His premise holds true for art as well as medicine.

Preferential tastes in art are a result of knowledge, time, age, experience, and many other circumstances. Taste in art is also a subjective preference, a gut reaction—what knocks you in the chest. Gut reactions based on knowledge and experience may also occur in medicine.

Art is an unrestricted communication—the expression of what the artist needs or wants to say and of the viewer's response to it. Doctors are constrained to deliver clear messages as conclusions—that is, what the patient needs to hear. Living is an art, and medicine is the art of making life a little better as it lasts a little longer. Art and medicine are two consequences of the same desire–to sustain life.

[Adapted from article in November 1990 *Minnesota Medicine*, ©1990 Minnesota Medical Association. Used by permission.]

Time

I have reached the age of awareness. A recent illness made me realize that the time of my life is limited. We all known this theoretically, but a serious illness makes it real. And when the theory becomes real, it alters our usual ways of thinking, feeling, and acting. As each passing day brings us closer to the end of life, we see the young and healthy among us ignoring the transience of human existence. We who are old and sick, however, cannot help but respond to it. We stand at a crossroads, and the turn we take will determine the quality of the time left to us.

One road leads to fear, hopelessness, and despair mingled with envy, resentment, and anger. It poisons our thoughts, spoils our personal relationships, and precludes any kind of involvement, productivity, or enjoyment. It decreases both the quality and the length of time left to us.

The other road leads to hope, courage, and joy mingled with generosity and sympathy. Its route encompasses an acceptance of our limitations and an appreciation of the impermanence of our existence. Once we accept our limitations, all our relationships and experiences are precious and fulfilling. Each taste, smell, and sight brings us pleasure. The joys and sorrows we share with fellow human beings renew our strength and affirm the desire to make the most of the gift of life. We become more outgoing and unselfish, more constructive and creative than ever. We are changed for the better in all physical and mental respects.

The choice between the positive and the negative is of crucial consequence to physicians and patients alike. The dictionary defines a physician as "a person skilled in the art of healing." We physicians can make our patients feel better and live longer—but only to a certain point. We are all subject to the laws of the universe whereby change is constant and all forms of life are impermanent. They have a beginning and end, and they undergo gradual transformation along the way. If we think about our transient existence in this context, then we can wisely consider our inevitable, individual deaths as a positive rather than negative phenomenon.

Physicians must minister to all kinds of patients—the temporarily and chronically afflicted, the acutely and terminally diseased. Our scientific education tells how long a typical patient in a certain stage of a given disease is likely to live. Our patients and their families expect us to provide them with this information. Yet as the information is transmitted from scientist to teacher, from teacher to physician, and from physician to patient, we often fail to consider that estimates of life expectancy are based on statistical averages that fail to take into account individual variations, attitudes, and therapies yet to be discovered or perfected. If we tell our patients only about their statistically probable life expectancies, we rob them of their individuality, erode their optimism, and, most grievously, conceal from them the prospects and rewards of choosing the road of positive feelings.

Physicians and patients must understand the wisdom of a positive response to the impermanence of human existence. Such an understanding benefits those whose lives are ending as well as the rest of us who fail to appreciate and enjoy even the most ordinary human experiences.

Medical students must receive a deeper grounding in theoretical and applied philosophy and psychology so as to help patients understand human life and lead rewarding lives. We doctors are obliged to offer our patients—young and old, curable and incurable, hopeful and hopeless— not only the most appropriate diagnostic and therapeutic procedures but also the help for appreciating and enjoying the time left to them.

Medical Humor Is No Laughing Matter

Soon after my arrival in the United States, I met distant relatives in New York. After a while, one of them turned to my brother and declared, "He laughs too much for a doctor."

I was amazed to learn that in my dream country, where everything is so abundant, rationing still existed for doctors' laughter.

In recent years, more articles in medical journals suggest doctors should reconsider old remedies such as herbs and spas and be open to new approaches such as biofeedback and acupuncture.

Therapies such as faith, music, pets, acupuncture, and massage are often beneficial when used with conventional treatment. Regardless of education, training, or philosophy, we doctors must agree that we cannot provide optimal care for our patients if we ignore everything except the direct cause and effect of the disease. We must consider the complexity of biological, mental, and environmental factors as well.

We know that alternative methods can also benefit mood. If stress can cause harm, can't harmony, peace, music, and color just as well improve our moods and well-being? When you hear a Beethoven violin concerto, see Monet's water lilies, smell spring flowers, or feel the warmth of the summer sun—aren't you experiencing mood enhancers?

Humor is an optimistic way to look at even tragic circumstances. Why not consider using it at appropriate times?

The sky over medical practice is stormy. We can be sad about it, ignore it, face it, or laugh about it. The situation remains the same, but our attitudes make all the difference in the way we feel.

From birth to death, life can be seen as a running down time or a mounting of experience. We can enjoy life or fear death. Humor acts as a set of rose-colored glasses, modifying the gray and blackness. Some people drink or take drugs to elevate their moods. Laughter is harmless and readily available. And it's free.

A positive attitude influences immunology in a positive way. Both laughter and chocolate promote the production of endorphins, which stimulate positive energy. I propose using more humor in our practice of daily life.

Doctors, please take humor seriously. Our most powerful tool is communication: the initial message, the presentation, and the diagnosis. Please do not wait until someone publishes a scientifically proven, double-blind study approved by the ethics committee, financially supported by the National Institutes of Health, and enthusiastically endorsed by the president of the United States. Acknowledge that humor has therapeutic value. Use it sooner—wherever and whenever it can help.

[Adapted from article in December 1998 *Minnesota Medicine*, © 1998 by Minnesota Medical Association. Used by permission.]

Reflections

It was −25 degrees F. in Minneapolis when the limousine picked me up to take me to the airport. In Tampa, where I arrived three hours later, it was 76 degrees F. At the baggage checkout, my luggage, with frost melting, seemed to perspire from the 100-degree change in temperature. I was to stay at the beautiful home of good friends and colleagues for a respite from the Minnesota winter.

Like water flowing over melting ice, thoughts passed through my mind on the colorful, sunny beach. Later, sitting on a bench, I viewed the mysterious night sky. Its vastness opens the imagination to contemplate infinity. Both close and distant stars were visible to the naked eye—all just a microscopic fraction of the unfolding, endless universe. The star "closest" to earth (excluding our sun) is 6,000,000,000,000 (6 trillion) miles away. The "closest" galaxy visible to the naked human eye is Andromeda—700,000 light years away, or 4,200,000,000,000,000,000 miles.

One can experience acrophobia (fear of height) from just a few feet above the ground, or from the window of a skyscraper, or from the top of a national park overlook. Yet we experience no dizziness, no space phobia, when contemplating the peaceful, distant, vast night sky. Is this deception—a visual misinterpretation by the brain—or just a means of protection from incomprehensible reality?

Looking through the transparent blue water, I notice a school of fish. The crowd is protection, security. Existence is average, safe. Rewards are minimal. Swimming alone is a risk, a choice, an adventure. The reward might be prosperity—or death. If one fish swims away and doesn't return, the others try to ignore it. ("It hasn't happened to me, has it? Or will it?") They swim away, jittery, without looking back.

A pelican glides above the waves, watching for fish, then suddenly dives into the water and comes up swallowing its catch. A brilliant flier, masterful fisher. A retired physician fishes on the dock, occasionally catching small fish. A pelican sits close by for hours, waiting patiently. If the fisherman accidentally drops a fish, the pelican picks it up immediately. These birds, though concerned about being caught, choose waiting rather than fishing for themselves. At some risk, they take the easy way. How does that apply to us?

At a shiny, heated outdoor swimming pool, old wrinkled bodies in bikinis exercise, fighting the inevitable—age and death—as if in a scene from a Fellini movie. Their inability or unwillingness to accept the inevitable opens the door to unhappiness.

At each age, beauty comes from a different source. Tight skin, big muscles, and physical beauty are not for most of the elderly. Wisdom and patience are rarely for the young. We must find the satisfactions of each age and time.

Health is a balance of the physical, spiritual, and environmental—a combination of physical and emotional well-being; an index of the mind based upon satisfaction with ourselves, our relationships with others, and their reflection upon us; a feeling of worth regarding human relationships, work, and recreation; an awareness of the beauty surrounding us and opportunities given to us, of the gift to be free and part of the universe; and an acceptance of the wonder of health and, at the same time, of its unimportance.

I brought my Florida friends a painting I had made. Painting is an immersion in nature, an ultimate ecstatic experience of creation. Facing the empty canvas brings an exciting sensation, like facing the night sky—thrilling moments for the mind contemplating infinite possibilities.

The world is a harmonious flow of forms and shapes ruled by the elegance of physical laws. Painting is merely a continuity of lines, shapes, colors, materials, and energy—the harmonic flow expressed visually. Painting is similar to the growth and development seen in children. It is a special branch of genetics.

In painting, I try to express how life could be rather than what it is. Colors are the notes of the visual symphony; they are the alphabet of joy. Someone once asked me how much time a painting takes. It has taken me 63 years of life experience, and I am merely a part of the continuity of another million years. Painting is a reflection of time.

[Adapted from article in July 1989 *Minnesota Medicine*, © 1989 by Minnesota Medical Association. Used by permission.]

Values

Treasures: Some years ago I took an unforgettable boat trip around the beautiful Greek Isles, including Crete and its Palace of Knossos, where the center of the Minoan civilization flourished in about 2000 B.C. Delightful frescoes of blue dolphins, flying fish, bulls, and acrobats are famous for influencing impressionist painters.

For their personal seals the Minoans used symbols such as the Christian cross, the Greek patriarchal cross, five- and six-pointed stars and the swastika—symbols that later took on broader identification.

A volcanic eruption caused a tidal wave of such magnitude that it wiped out all Minoan life and artifacts. When I visited Knossos, the treasury of the King's palace held six pieces of crushed metal weighing no more than a few pounds. Five thousand years ago these were their most treasured items.

Stradivarius: Antonio Stradivarius is universally regarded as the greatest of all violinmakers. His instruments have an incredible richness of tone and the ability to respond to the musician with an ample reserve of power. Seven hundred of his instruments are known to exist today.

In 1954, after the completion of medical training, I commuted by train between my home in Budapest and the mining town of Tatabánya, where I worked as a family practitioner. On the train I met many others who, like me, were forced to work outside the city because we were considered the ideological enemies of the Communist system.

For the first time I was making enough money to be able to buy more than the essentials. At 29 years of age, I had saved enough to buy my first tailor-made suit. One of my traveling companions was a lawyer who had been one of the top prosecutors in the Hungarian judicial system; now, however, he worked as a clerk in a collective. One day he told me that a Stradivarius violin was for sale. It probably had been stolen from the Eszterházy estate during the Russian occupation. The Eszterházy family was known for centuries as one of the richest landholders. The members of the family were supporters of the arts; Haydn lived on their estate. In the 17th century, they built an opera house visited by all the important musicians at the time.

Since I played violin, I went to see the Stradivarius. The old case revealed a beautiful bow and a magnificent instrument. Through the F-hole, I saw the engraved Stradivarius name. How much? The asking price was the amount I had saved for my suit. I had waited for so long to buy the suit, which I did. Musical experts consider Stradivarius violins to be priceless.

～

Irises: Vincent van Gogh developed an expression of rhythmic line and turned colors and textures into a dynamic personal experience. He suffered many ailments,

and his life was mostly influenced by manic depression—
"like the suffering of the oyster producing a pearl."

Van Gogh's suffering produced some of the most profound paintings during his short but memorable life. His well-preserved letters describe the creation of each of his paintings and the fact that during his lifetime he sold only one painting—for 40 francs—even though his supportive brother was an influential Parisian art dealer. In the final weeks of his life, when fame caught up with his brilliance, Van Gogh was already beyond the frivolousness of earthly recognition. His suffering reached a crescendo, and he killed himself.

Nearly 100 years after Van Gogh's death, a collector bought his *Irises* for $50 million, at that time the largest amount of money ever paid for a painting.

Lipstick: When you walk through the cosmetics section of a department store, you see lipsticks lined up like colorful flowers of the meadow, tempting and attracting women with their many shades and hues.

I have seen the darkest place on earth in the shadow of misery, where people had nothing less than bare existence. Even so, despite the searches and confiscations gold pieces—symbols of the only buying power in a German concentration camp—remained hidden. Amazingly, some people even had lipstick for sale; the price was one French Napoleon gold piece. It was sold not for making lips more exciting, but for its flavor, for making lips less hungry.

Medals: Oh, how beautiful to see the colorful, sparkling medals exchanged by leaders of the world! How ridiculous to see the Russian generals, whose plentiful decorations covered both sides of their uniforms. Some might wonder whether they had more medals—attached to the seats of their pants.

A few years ago it was fashionable to use military medals on women's jackets. I was traveling in Europe and looking for a gift for my wife. I went to an antique shop. Hundreds of iron, bronze, and silver medals from World Wars I and II were on display. Looking at the medals, I saw suffering, pain, blood, and unfulfilled dreams. I imagined honor and pride, decency and idealism, responsibility and duty, a pat on the shoulder, an attempt to straighten as the medals were pinned on. I could hear the drums and music, the speeches and the cheers. I envisioned a handshake for the widow, a hug for the orphans and tears.

A decade later, the medals were sold for pennies.

Example: A scholarly rabbi once was asked, "What are the three most important things to give a child?"

His answer: "Example, example, and example."

["Values" adapted from article in March 1990 *Minnesota Medicine*, © 1990 by Minnesota Medical Association. Used by permission.].

Thoughts on Food

So many TV commercials focus on different ways to lose weight. The social pressure on people to lose pounds is overwhelming, and slimness has become the hallmark of beauty. Billions of dollars are spent (mostly in vain) on losing fat for social advantage. This social pressure has now reached those in medical circles as well. (I've never seen a slim dietitian!)

Articles, insurance charts, and statistics seem focused on how different nutrients may be beneficial or detrimental in the fight against fat. Today the customer expects to pay a high price for tasteless, unappealing, but healthy "organic" mishmash. Meanwhile, the host and hostess of a gourmet dinner apologize to their guests in advance for the "unhealthy" ingredients in their feast.

I have heard that the success rate for obese people losing weight is no better than the cure rate for lung cancer— about 3 percent. I attended a symposium at which young residents presented obesity as a disease simply requiring the control of a concerned physician and a dietitian. Nothing could be further from reality.

Watch a nature program on television, and what do you see? The animal parents supply food, and the offspring eats and eats. When it grows up, it attacks, eats, and stores within its body (and elsewhere) more food than it needs. When you watch your child eat, you have a warm feeling of being a provider. The more you can provide the better. Every day I see parents from many parts of the world whose only concern for their healthy growing children is that the children do not eat well. Very rarely is a parent concerned because a child eats too much.

I see children with PKU from their very first week of life. They all eat some artificial foods, and the amounts are based on the child's weight. Later some of the children are obese and some are slim; some have small heads and some large. This suggests that the differences are caused by genetically dominant forces rather than by the intake of specific foods. The percentage of obese PKU children is similar to that of non-PKU children, in spite of more precise control and education concerning their diets.

When you reach for peanuts while watching a game or a snack between meals, you are not eating because you are hungry. And when you eat something pleasant, you often don't stop when you are full. An inner urge forces you to eat more than you really need. The natural desire is not to stop but to continue eating. This is not a weakness. It is a genetically determined, chemically enforced, physiological function.

We have a built-in need to feed ourselves beyond what is essential. When food becomes less readily available, the body's requirement decreases so as to protect and maintain the balance of energy and to urge the body to obtain more food. We want to eat more because our built-in instinct is to prepare for a time when food might not be available or when we might have a disease. Recent studies have shown that mildly obese people have a better chance of recovery from disease than slim people.

Besides, eating is one of our most common sensual pleasures.

Thus the attempt to counteract obesity through diet is likely doomed to fail. Biologically and genetically we are built for an environment of the past, one in which food was not as close as the neighborhood grocery and people obtained food through struggle. Today one of the difficulties in industrialized countries is that food is both abundant and inexpensive. In the primitive past the only task was for every living creature to find food every day.

We still, automatically, want to eat as much as possible. Our stomachs urge us to eat more and more, while our educated brain tries to coax us into eating less. (Constantly changing information about the value of particular ingredients further confuses us.) There is a conflict between the biological desire to eat and the intellectual objection to quantity. The first is ancient and ingrained, and the second is recent and learned. In modern days many of us have been able to get food so easily, so inexpensively, without physical work: the consequence is increasing obesity.

Besides being genetically programmed to eat to store and conserve energy, we tend to move in energy-saving ways. I observed this one winter day at the Como Park Zoo while watching a polar bear swimming. The bear's motions were monotonous. He pushed himself down through the water with his right rear foot, then came straight up from below using his left rear foot, then turned on his back and repeated the motion again and again without changing his routine, pace, or timing in the slightest. He used the least energy and the shortest route every time. Similarly, a predator attacks if the effort of the kill will require less energy than what it can expect to gain in nutrient value from the prey; otherwise, it gives up the chase.

Human beings also tend to be efficient in many of their movements. I have noticed that in the office, the kitchen, and the bathroom—everywhere, day and night, people work out routines for the shortest or fastest ways, which then become almost automatic. We follow the same steps and go through the same processes to perform daily activities most efficiently and with the least effort. And we take shortcuts—for example, moving diagonally across a space instead of going around a corner. We want to conserve energy, so we simplify and automate our activities; we do it most effectively when establishing a familiar pattern that requires no conscious thought.

Because many of our eating and moving behaviors are automatic, we need to spend more time and energy on exercise and diet. I once heard a radio announcer say that if you do appropriate exercises and eat the right foods, an autopsy will not able to identify the cause of your death.

But until we learn the actual biological mechanisms and correct nutritional requirements, our concern should not be how to die but how to live.

[Adapted from article in July 1992 *Minnesota Medicine*, © 1992 by Minnesota Medical Association. Used by permission.]

Religion

I was born and raised by my parents in traditional Jewish fashion. But from my early infancy, a devoted Catholic named Anna lived in our home and took care of me. Religion was a dominating factor in my life. Through my youth, the Bible ruled and directed my identity in every aspect of life. I sincerely believed that even a simple thing like touching or not touching a table was God's wish and direction. I could not do anything without His knowledge, due to of His eternal presence.

I was 19 years old when the Germans occupied Hungary. I was taken to a concentration camp and survived. My brother was in Switzerland during the war. My mother survived by hiding in the home of Anna's parents. The Nazis killed my father and all of my relatives. Religion did not matter to me anymore. It seemed to me that the ever-present God had taken a long nap. Religions seemed to be an additional barrier—like race, nationality, and class.

I did not become bitter or filled with hate; I just lost my childhood idealism. I lived by the same principles as before, not to please God or because of God's judgment but because I could not and still cannot find a more appropriate way to act toward others than what I learned as a child.

I do not seek the company of or identify myself with similar nationals, religious groups, or professionals. I identify and share my time and thoughts with those whose values are similar to mine.

A joke I heard as a child in Budapest goes like this:

Two Jews are talking, and one says "I am proud to be Jewish."

The other man asks why.

The first man replies, "Because even if I was not proud, I would still be a Jew. So I might as well be proud of it."

That is the way I am and will always be—a Jew. This is my destination not by choice but by circumstance. I do not consider my religion to be superior to other faiths. It is the way I was born and raised, and it has had an unchangeable effect on me. Like the color of my skin or hair—that is the way I am. But as my hair color changes from black to gray, my insides are maturing, and I see values and religion differently from the way I did in the past.

In the last year, I've discovered two new resources influencing my view of religion, God, and our way of life. The first is the Jewish philosopher Maimonides. He has written that God's royalty is his essence and not his function. He is a transcendent God, the God who is beyond anything that exists in human awareness.

In other words, God cannot be understood by the human mind. Believing in Him cannot be based upon whether He created us in His image. Our faith must be unconditional—God's presence or absence has nothing to do what may be happening with us. My actions must be based not on concern about His judgment of me but on my human responsibility. Faith and its practice are, at the first level, above primitive biology. God, to me, is the ultimate, and I am grateful to witness a little part of His immense, eternal domain.

The other major influence on my own spiritual life is

Buddha. His concept of religion was purely ethical. He cared everything about conduct and nothing about ritual, worship, metaphysics, or theology.

He said, "An atom can never understand the cosmos."

Saintliness and content lie not in knowledge of the universe and God but simply in selfless and beneficent living. Buddha offers a religion absolutely free of dogma and priest craft and proclaims a way of salvation open to infidels and believers alike.

"It is foolish to suppose that another can cause us happiness or misery," says Buddha. "These are always the product of our own behavior and our desires. In the end, we perceive the absurdity of moral and psychological individualism. Our fretting selves are not really separate beings and powers, but passing ripples on the stream of life, little knots forming and unraveling in the wind-blown mesh of fate. When we see ourselves as parts of whole, when we reform our selves and our desires in terms of the whole, then our personal disappointments and defeats, our varied suffering and inevitable death, no longer sadden us as bitterly as before, they are lost in the amplitude of infinity. When we have learned to love not our separate life, but all men and all living things, then at last we shall find peace."

In other words, the measure of my virtue is the way I treat others—independent of the existence of a spiritual or a specifically outlined religion.

But my conduct is also based upon an old tradition. The Jewish tradition formed me and I formed it in me, over time and through my witness of some of the world's worst inhumanity to man changing my childish faith to belief. It forced me to blame not God, but those with human faces who perpetrated the primitive, hateful, murderous acts I saw. I learned that I could act humanely not only because I belonged to a religious group but also because that is my only appropriate role here and now—"to remain humane in any circumstances."

Many godless acts have been committed in the name of God. Let us not use His name in vain but act justly for the sake of others and for ourselves. To be respected, we must respect others. We must use religion not as a shield but as way of helping.

[Adapted from Robert Fisch, "Jewish by Destiny," *Turtle River Press*, April 1997).]

Holiday Gifts

A First and Last Christmas

When I arrived in Minneapolis in June 1958 to join the pediatrics department at the University of Minnesota, I saw a sign that said, "You are approaching the Twin Cities, home of the University of Minnesota and Dayton's." I had heard the Minnesota had extremely cold weather, so one of my first stops was Dayton's Department Store.

"I would like to buy a storm coat," I told a salesman.

After searching in the storage room, he eventually brought out a coat and asked me where I was going.

"I'm staying here."

Well, the winter came. My shiny "new" used car began to smoke on the first freezing morning. After I had several accidents, my chief resident quipped, "You know, Bob, those red, yellow, and green lights on the street corners are not Christmas decorations."

I remained enthusiastic about driving, however, and when a college student was willing to risk going to dinner with me, I happily took her out in a snowstorm. I did not have the vaguest notion where to go, and after an hour of driving, I found an elegantly lit building and pointed it out as my favorite restaurant. It was a funeral home.

But my real story is about the little girl I first met at the university hospital under the usual circumstances. When I arrived at her bedside to collect blood, tears were streaming down her cheeks. With her curly blond hair and large amethyst eyes, she looked like an angel, but her face was covered with bruises, the signs of her abusive malignancy. There was no smile on her face, only sadness, and her eyes expressed the tiredness of a chronic sufferer. She was not looking forward but looking backward, collecting some traces of better memories from the past.

Still, her expression of sorrow and beauty reminded me of *The Pieta*, and I felt what we doctors feel when, at the end of our medical resources, we reach a mixture of frustration and powerlessness—when diminishing medical possibilities must be balanced by increasing compassion, when we search for answers that medical knowledge fails to provide, when we helplessly confront the inevitable. I called her "Angel."

We became friends. She began to serve as my interpreter (she understood my heavily accented English) during morning rounds, and when evening came and everyone else had gone, I sat at her bedside holding her left hand (her right arm had been amputated), and we told each other stories.

Through our stories we met again, and tears flowed again from our eyes. I told her about Budapest—the hilliness of Buda and the flatness of Pest—divided by the

Danube (never blue), which I always saw through my window. The city has thermal waters beneath it and thus the only zoo in the world where a hippopotamus can have offspring. The hippos keep their big mouths open, and the children pretzels throw in. I told her about the Gypsies there, wandering from place to place telling fortunes from cards and palms and playing the violin so beautifully, though they were never taught in school.

I told her about Budapest, the city I loved and had to leave. She told me about her family's farm—the dogs and ponies—her grandfather (who talked funny, like me), her sister, daddy, and mommy, school, games, and toys, and above all, Christmas—the tree, the dresses, the songs and the colorful, gift-wrapped boxes. Her exquisite face radiated joy as memory momentarily defeated suffering. Then her tears fell like snowflakes as she thought again of the farm, where she could not be.

There was no cure for her; transfusions only prolonged her agony. Her one desire was to be in her home and to die there, and the doctors and her parents agreed she should have this wish. I told her she could go home for Christmas. Her face was radiant with joy. Her eyes sparkled, her pain temporarily abated. Going out the door, she turned back: "Happy Christmas, Dr. Fisch! I will send you something special."

Every Christmas evening since then, when I look out the window and see the mysterious light and falling snow and hear the wind blow in the coldness of solitude, her gentle face appears in my memory, bringing warmth, and I hear again her everlasting good wishes. Though many years have passed since then, I feel still closer every Christmas. Angel's gift to me is remarkable. She made Christmas into a day that reminds me again that life, health, and the smile of a child are not to be taken for granted.

When I hear children laugh, I feel life and growth around me. I am grateful for the chance to have them around, to be their doctor, to make them feel better, even though the gaiety may be their last. I am happy to watch my daughter, Alexandria, and others develop, to see their new knowledge and human understanding grow each year, to see the quality of life improve so that all our children will live more fully than generations before.

My Angel gave me a special meaning for Christmas. She taught me that every day is special. Children make us aware of our limitations, including that of our short existence, so that every experience becomes more precious and fulfilling.

The Gift of God

I first heard the phrase from an Egyptian mother who lovingly watched her newborn's warm, dark eyes and joyful face: "Doctor, she is a gift of God." I have heard this statement and said it to myself many times since then.

The boy was nearly eight years old when he returned to the hospital. His face was unrecognizable because of his pain, the marks of his disease, and the side effects of the drugs he was taking. The continuing failure of medical intervention had erased any hope for a cure. At their last supper, the father said grace: "We thank God for each minute we are together. Time is the gift of God."

Her mother's history had revealed surgery for carcinoma of the thyroid. She was delicate, with her mother's face. Sometime later I received a letter from the grandmother, who had had a tumor of the adrenal gland. I took it to my friend and colleague, Dr. Robert Gorlin, a remarkable human being and walking memory bank. After glancing at the first line of the letter, he told me that this family had multiple mucosal neuroma syndrome, a genetic disease. The girl had a 50 percent chance for malignancy, but early detection could prevent disaster.

After I met with the parents and discussed this with them, the mother said, "Dr. Gorlin's knowledge is the gift of God."

At one time in my life, I was in a place where the presence of starving skeletons visually reminded me of the darkness of humanity. The sounds I heard in the concentration camp were the moans of the dying, the screams of prisoners, and the gunfire of SS guards.

One day an unusual thing happened. Capos working with the SS were distributing Red Cross packages there. Often they took the goods in the packages themselves. I once saw a guard eat a whole big bar of chocolate by himself. At the time of the distribution, I was barely able to walk; I received two cubes of sugar as my portion! Have you ever seen celebrities, with their huge diamonds reflecting rarity, beauty, wealth, and privilege? I looked at the sugar cubes as if they were from another world—a world where food has only nutritional value and is abundantly available—a world farther away from me than another universe. I could not admire the beauty of the shiny crystals for long; I gobbled them up. The sweet flavor overwhelmed me, and tears fell from my eyes. As strength flowed to my weak body from those cubes of sugar, I realized that food is the gift of God.

The Art Institute of Chicago has a Renoir painting called *The Two Sisters*. It shows two young girls on a terrace surrounded by flowers, trees, a lake, and a chateau. The young faces, the soft lines, and the streaming light capture the beauty of a moment in the girls' lives, preserving it for others to appreciate. The artist's talent is a gift from God.

When driving at dawn in the morning traffic, I turn on my radio and listen to Mozart. It lifts me from the hustle of daily existence, and my spirit flies with the brilliant notes of that musical genius. Two hundred years ago, the child Mozart created music providing enjoyment for generation after generation—a timeless acoustical pleasure. The sound of music, too, is a gift from God.

A young woman was twenty-one years old and pregnant. Everything was progressing according to her hopes and dreams when, in the third month of her pregnancy, a node biopsy revealed the presence of malignancy, the fourth stage of Hodgkin's disease. Her doctor recommended abortion and radiation to save her life. She would most likely live, and she might become pregnant again, though this could not be predicted with certainty. She made her decision immediately and without hesitation. This might be her only chance to give life as it one was given. She carried her pregnancy to full term and delivered a healthy baby girl.

Before she died, two weeks after the birth, she told me while hugging her infant, "So many claim the importance of different creations and discoveries, yet the utmost achievement performed daily by millions of mothers is giving birth. Life, the gift of God, as given through me to my child."

⌒

A three-year-old's chocolate-brown face lit up when I entered the examination room. She was chewing a cookie.

"Hi, Dr. Fisch," she said with a smile. "Would you like my cookie?" She took it out of her mouth and handed it to me. In her gesture I felt her love—the gift of God.

⌒

A young PKU patient was graduating from college. His older, PKU sister attended the ceremony in a wheelchair. She could not walk or say even a single word.

Twenty-five years earlier, I had traveled on a harsh winter morning to a small town in northern Minnesota soon after the young man was born. I took a blood sample to determine early whether he had the same diagnosis as his sister. Her mental challenges had alerted us to the hereditary disorder. Her illness was the price paid for her brother's early diagnosis. That was before newborns were routinely screened for PKU.

Because the boy's blood showed a high phenylalanine level, we started him on a special diet, which allowed him to grow up strong physically and mentally. To be able to help this child was a gift from God.

⌒

I was tired, and it was hard to make it up the steps of the National Gallery of Art in Washington, D.C. Fear and sorrow darkened my mind. Then I saw a Monet paining from the Hermitage—a woman in a white dress standing with a parasol in the middle of a flower garden. The colors of the flowers radiated the joy of life and brought fresh air into the exhibition hall. As I inhaled the air and absorbed the light, my inner darkness and fear diminished. The artist's masterpiece opened my eyes to life's abundant joys and rewards. That creation of beauty led me to recover from the darkness of my depression. Joy is a gift of God.

⤫

They came from a small village. Friends since childhood, they both had been separated from their parents for a long time. They knew nothing and had nothing but each other. During the last month of the war they walked through the Alps and over the mountain passes in the ultimate test of endurance. At the time I met them, they were two 16-year-olds, walking skeletons. They had to keep marching through the snowy winter, without food or water; the SS guards would shoot anyone who sat down to rest. The boys walked holding hands. One was blind, and the other was his guide. It was more than a year since they had left home. Their friendship kept them alive. Their friendship was a gift from God.

⤫

We could barely crawl from weakness. Time was distorted reality; minutes seemed to be months. Our tired bodies were close to the ultimate exhaustion—death. Starvation altered our senses. The meaning of life was lost. Human desires narrowed to simple reflex. We heard the news that the American army was coming to liberate us. A few young, strong soldiers arrived in a jeep. A new life began. Our freedom was a gift of God.

[Adapted from an article in December 1991 Minnesota Medicine ©1992 by Minnesota Medical Association. Used by permission.]

Giving Brings a Spirit of Enlightenment

The holy days of winter comprise a season of contemplation—for some, the story of the three kings traveling to Bethlehem. For others it is a season of light during the longest period of darkness or the presence of children filled with joyful excitement. For all of us, warm memories melt the harshness of winter.

The season can be a celebration of human enlightenment for those who feel the need for something beyond everyday existence, for something beyond material things—who believe human relationships are more than give and take, that some way of life might remain as illumination for others, just as the Northern Lights give hope in the face of the darkness of doubt, just as the candles of Christmas and Hanukkah give witness to the spirit and to our for the future.

The snowflakes fall peacefully from the sky on a late December evening. As I look through my window toward St. Anthony Falls on the Mississippi River, a recurrent of thought flows through my mind. When someone walks barefoot on the seashore, the waves gradually wash away the footprints, regardless of how deep they might be. Most of our actions and materials—our existence—eventually fade away without leaving a trace.

I have always been keenly aware of time, but in the presence of a few exceptional people offering spiritual enrichment, time could become nonexistent. I could listen to their stories and watch their daily activities endlessly. Even when we were together no longer, they remained with me, and their presence made a mark upon me. Their personalities, words, and deeds cut to my soul, and I will carry those marks so long live.

Who are my kings? Actually, I have one queen and three kings. Let me introduce them to you:

My queen's name is Anna. She was 18 years old when she came to our home. I was just eight months when she came to be my nanny. My mother and father worked more than 12 hours every weekday and five hours on Sunday. Anna became a member of our family. When she died at age 80, she was the last to live in our home in Budapest, which she kept as it had been many years before.

At age 22, Ann became very sick; she was bedridden and in a body cast for a year. From then on, every step was a hardship. But her physical handicap was not noticeable, and a gentle personality and kindness emanated from her deep Catholicism.

She was always with me. Not only did we spend time and play together in the beautiful gardens of Budapest, but every Sunday I sat next to her during Mass—as natural for me as it was for her to celebrate all the Jewish holidays in our home. From Anna I learned tolerance, kindness, and all the fundamentals a boy could ever need.

When I turned 18 in 1944, I was taken to a labor camp. My mother was hiding in Anna's family home. In December 1944, Budapest was nearly surrounded by the Russian army. I was in a village 20 miles from the German border, facing cold, snow, isolation, and the constant question, "What next?" And "When?"

Late one dreary afternoon, a limping figure appeared in the gray snow beyond the barbed-wire fence. Anna had come; she had begged the guard to let her see me? I hugged her and kissed the gentle face of the one who had brought light in the darkness, hope in the time of greatest despair.

She brought a little food. Oh, how much that meant to me, the food she had saved for me by denying herself! She brought a wool blanket to keep me warm. I promised that if I stayed alive, I would bring it back.

I learned afterwards that she had taken the last train before the surrender of Budapest, hanging onto the crowded train steps, risking her life to bring me bread and hope and warmth. I returned the blanket as promised; her warmth remains with me all my days.

~

My first king is Uncle Kazi. He had silvery hair, always wore a smile, and spoke kind, soft words. I first met him when I arrived as a district doctor in the Hungarian mining town of Tatabánya. He was my superior, the head of the Public Health Department. In the years following, I was fortunate to win his friendship.

His father was a wealthy landlord in the most fertile area of the country. The estate had belonged to their family for centuries. Despite the customary separation of economic classes in those days, all the workers on Kazi's land ate lunch at his large dining table in the mansion; his father cut the meat and served everyone personally.

Uncle Kazi was a legend in the town. When the Communist authorities tried to prosecute him, an open street protest freed him in an unprecedented episode of the Communist regime.

Each summer Uncle Kazi spent his vacation in his summer home at Tihany, the most beautiful spot on Lake Balaton. The house, worn by time and a lack of money for repairs, no longer displayed its original elegance and grandeur. It faced the lake, and birches lined the road on both sides. Uncle Kazi and his wife, Ilike, took their favorite Puli (sheepdog) and all their domestic animals—including chickens, ducks—with them on vacation. They never killed or ate any of the fowl, which roamed freely in the house.

Next to the house was a large building with a beautiful garden, used by the employees of the Hungarian National

Bank for free two-week summer vacations. Once I was visiting Uncle Kazi, and after a delicious dinner, we sat on the balcony of his house, enjoying the sunset and a light breeze. I asked about the building next door—who had built it and when?

"Oh, that was mine. We built it as a private, 24-bed sanatorium before the World War II. The Communists nationalized it."

"That was yours? Aren't you upset by such an injustice? When you see the building day in and day out, aren't you irritated?" I asked.

Uncle Kazi looked at me with his gentle smile and said, "You know, my dear friend Robi, this way it might be enjoyed better by so many more."

⌒⤬

I first met Robert Rosenthal, my second king, during my internship at Children's Hospital in St. Paul. Although he was a solo practitioner until his retirement at age 86, he had the energy and insight to become one of the best-known medical historians, collectors, and scholars. Above all, he was a sensitive, kind, giving, human being.

Dr. Rosenthal's wife frequently accompanied him on house calls. Leaving Children's Hospital late one evening, he told his wife of his despair over a little boy who had been uninterested in food for days and was dying. At that time, IV solutions and hyper alimentation were unknown, and the child's prognosis was grave.

Late that evening Mrs. Rosenthal started making cookies in various shapes, and at 1 A.M. Dr. Rosenthal brought the cookies to the child. The little boy opened his eyes, smiled, and reached for the cookies.

Through his medical knowledge Dr. Rosenthal was able to many patients well and to translate medical wisdom and history from Latin, Hebrew, German and other cultures to many others. He was an endless source of information on trees, drugs, customs, legends and stories, which he loved to share with friends.

⟡

The king above all others was my father, who radiated love and compassion. His way of life honored high values and human relationships in the finest way. To live with him was like being in a fairytale world—there gentleness overwhelmed power, kindness removed rudeness, and giving made it unnecessary to ask. Once a refugee musician needed a dinner jacket for performances; without question, my father bought one for him. At the market where my father worked, not a day passed without someone looking for help—money, food, or clothing—I never saw him turn someone away. He gave effortlessly. His favorite motto was: "Live and let live."

The world then used another motto, that of final solution: "Erase them." Seeing hungry inmates when he arrived at a termination camp, my father shared his last meal, saying, "I always have enough." Even the most extreme human brutality did not alter his way of living, though it took his life away. He is gone, yet he provided me with guidance about how to live as a human being in every circumstance.

⟡

What did my queen and kings have in common? They did not look for external reward; their wealth was in their nature, and giving made them richer. The joy of giving brought them enlightenment.

Think about your own kings and queens—your loved ones, friends, and others you care for or who need your help. Their presence and memory enlighten your heart, as candles light our rooms on special days. May all of us, in our work and in our lives, have a positive impact on others. May traces of our footprints remain.

[Adapted from an article in December 1992 Minnesota Medicine © 1992 Minnesota Medical Association]

The Magic Touch

As light from the sun illuminates the universe, this image lights my memory: Michelangelo's depiction of God's finger touching the finger of Adam on the ceiling of the Sistine Chapel, in Rome. When I first entered that pinnacle of beauty, I was so overwhelmed that the only way to express my feeling was to fall to my knees, something I had never done before. It was not just a matter of symbolism. The "touch" emits a flow of love and power.

The image of that touch is always with me. Fortunately, I have experienced many other touches, and although they were not so widely recognized, they are of no less importance to me than that of the great Italian master.

Family Touching. As was customary in many Budapest families before a meal, I kissed the bread and kissed my parents and thanked them for my food. Whenever anyone came into or went out of the house, we kissed. Lovers, and friends too, held each other's hands when they walked. Physical touch with others became part of my nature.

I could not comprehend when in the famous story (and movie) *The Fighting Sullivans* five members left home to fight in World War II without a hug or kiss for their father. I understand that social behaviors and customs differ according to culture, yet it seems inconceivable that people deny themselves expression of joy, sorrow, thanks, friendship, or farewell.

I understand that a baby monkey feels security in touching its mother's tail; otherwise it feels panicky. My first act when I enter an examination room is to make contact with the child; in the case of a young child, I usually touch the arm or stroke the hair. A patient/doctor relationship without human contact cannot be considered complete.

~~~

The Helping Hand: Early on the morning of June 3, 1944, my father and I arrived at a corner near our home where the streetcar stopped. A heavy backpack over my shoulder contained all the materials I was allowed to take to the labor camp. The heaviest burden, however, was carried not on my shoulders but in our hearts. We realized that these sad moments might be our last ones together. And they were.

When the streetcar arrived, we kissed each other—not to say goodbye but to stay together as long as possible. From behind me, my father's hand lifted my backpack as I stepped on the stairs. According to the laws of physics, a body whose motion is initiated by power travels eternally in space. I still feel my father's hand lightening my burden, sending me on.

~~~

Weight of Responsibility: The girl was 12 years old and complained of a sore throat. I had never met her before, but somehow the complaint did not account for her obvious, deep sadness. I asked the aunt who accompanied her for an explanation.

They had arrived from Ethiopia six months before. The previous week, her father had lost his job and committed suicide. In his last note, he asked his young daughter to preserve the family. The father could not bear the thought her losing his support. He left behind dignity and pride. Touched by his last message and remembering his lifetime example of responsibility, his daughter became painfully aware of what now was her responsibility. That knowledge already burdened her youthful face.

Carrying His Child: I could hardly believe my eyes when I saw a small Asian man walking into the clinic with a large, unresponsive child in his arms.

"His son has a cold," the interpreter translated.

When they left, the father was barely able to carry the boy, yet somehow he managed. The look of kindness on his rugged old face reminded me of the famous *Pieta* of Michelangelo—the gentle, radiant, loving face of the Madonna gazing upon the dead son in her arms. I learned later that the child had earlier suffered severe brain as the result of an accident. Since then, although the father had many children older and younger, this child, who needed his attention and loving touch more than the others, had become his father's favorite.

Free to Touch the Wall: When I went to the Wailing Wall in Jerusalem, I dressed according to religious law. At first when I saw those famous, old stones, I felt nothing. I just stood there motionless. But when I faced the old stones and touched them, I suddenly realized I was the first and only one in my family who, after many generations and a millennium, had fulfilled the deepest desire of my ancestors to be in Jerusalem as a free man. Then I cried like a baby.

I was grateful for this privilege, and I prayed that my child and her child and others would remain free in the generations to come.

Courier to Bethlehem: "I am only a messenger. I came to pay homage in the name of Anna. As you know, she cannot come. She is crippled. And all the suffering she has gone through year after year, when even a single motion is painful, does not stop her from praying to you for hours every day at dawn and at night. She is indeed your devoted servant. I just want to thank you myself for the love and kindness she has given me since my early childhood." And then when no one could see, for her I touched and kissed what is known as the birthplace of Jesus in a temple in Bethlehem.

At the Time of Despair: I was alone. If anyone else was there, he was light years away. I felt only insignificance; I was a burden. And I was facing a surgical procedure. The fear that had been so much a part of my life was now apathy. The doctors were occupied with preparing their instruments and had no time to chat me. An elderly black aide held me and squeezed my arm once, to say, "I understand. I am with you." Then warmth and hope surged within me.

Since then I have tried to provide for others something similar to the touch that she provided in the darkest moment of my life. We should always try to touch others—by our presence, communication, work, attitude, actions, and words. The impact of my touch, your touch, may not reach a zenith like that of a world master, yet its intent is the same and it may shine on the recipient like Michelangelo's touch of God's finger did on me.

The Power of Sound, Words, and Music

Sound: I listen to the faint sounds of St. Anthony Falls on the Mississippi River through the closed window of my apartment. The river is a constant reminder of the flow of time.

Producing and perceiving sound occupies a major portion of our lives. Within the mother's womb a constant pulsation of the aorta is a comfort to the developing embryo. The audible heartbeat of the embryo is a milestone of pregnancy, reassurance of appropriate development. The first cry of the newborn is a loud announcement: "I have arrived. I am here!" The perception and learning of language is the most significant part of human development. The cry of a loved one at the bedside of one dying is the last sound before eternal silence.

Although we often comment on the preciousness of our eyes and our sight, we seem to appreciate less our ears and the gift of hearing. Most of our learning comes through sound. People react impatiently to the limitations of the hearing impaired but go out of their way to assist those who are visually handicapped. Yet it has been shown that blindness does not interfere with the normal intellectual development of a child, while deafness does.

━━━

Words: After the birth of an infant, verbal reassurance by the doctor that the newborn thrives brings noticeable relief and joyful satisfaction to the mother, after at least nine months of waiting, nourishing, and worrying.

Then follow the consequences of the birth of a child to a family.

Likewise the tired but encouraging voice of the surgeon melts away the tension from the faces of anxious relatives. Their relief is combined with hope for the continuation of existence rather than its sudden interruption or the end. The devastating news of an incurable disease is not only the beginning of the recognition that death is inevitable, but also the first tear in the fabric of family, friendship, and other relationships. The hard trip toward complete aloneness and the unknown begins.

During my obstetrical training, I learned to practice hypnosis. We used it for relieving pain. The appropriate atmosphere for hypnosis requires that both the subject and the environment be relaxed; the crucial ingredient is the trust of the patient in hearing the message. The hypnotist says what the subject wants to hear.

Following each session, the hypnotist suggests a task (for example, "You will not be able to leave the room until you hear two claps"). One patient told me that she felt better afterwards and was ready to leave. She put her hand on the doorknob but waited for the two claps before she opened the door.

When I first attended a hypnosis session, I could not believe what was taking place right in front of my eyes. Under hypnosis complete surgeries can be performed without anesthetizing the patient.

What a shame that today we talk about providers and consumers, that second opinions and suspicion have replaced the trust between doctor and patient, reducing considerably the effectiveness of therapy. Patients look at the side effects or potential damages of treatment rather than expecting to feel better from it.

A dietitian friend and her missionary husband lived in New Guinea. Her letters to me, both in substance and in their surprise endings, were as fascinating as the novels of Somerset Maugham. She wrote a few times about the village witch doctor. Women in the village, after having enough children, asked his help to prevent their having more. He gave them something to take by mouth (this was before birth-control pills), and it worked. Australian researchers took samples for analysis and found out that it was nothing more than a little piece of earth mixed in water.

The witch doctors were also able to predict the day of someone's death. Naturally fear and absolute trust contribute greatly to the results of prediction. Each of us has the ability to convey messages, teach, educate, modify, change, build on, or ruin existing ideas. We have the all-powerful tool of communication—the most powerful natural human weapon. Hitler, with his inflammatory and powerful speeches, mesmerized a civilized nation that went on to destroy more than 50 million human beings. At the other extreme, Mother Teresa has with her kindness healed countless suffering souls.

～✦

Music: The first four notes of Beethoven's Fifth Symphony are probably the most widely recognized musical motif in the world. It is the hallmark of human musical genius, endlessly and repeatedly glorifying not only its creator but also all who hear it. The powerful sound of these famous four notes renews strength, reflects endless zest, and suggests optimism for the present and future of humanity. Like an echo of the Big Bang, it will reverberate as long as the universe lasts, a resonance of the unlimited human spirit.

Music is like the sound waves of which it is made; it

spreads out and is unrestricted by conventional bound-aries. No single word can even come close to expressing the limitless influence of music everywhere and through all time.

Research confirms that college students' test perfor-mance improves after the students are exposed to classi-cal music. Ecstatic audiences at symphony halls and rock concerts around the world provide overwhelming evi-dence of the importance of music in the lives of human beings. Music is ever present on radio and television, in homes and cars, from speakers in shopping centers, on the phone while one is on "hold"—a perpetual proof of the influence of sound and music.

The sound of the falls, the power of words, can be construc-tive or destructive, used for love or for hate, spoken with anger or with joy. We must be careful to choose our words for the benefit of everyone—for laughing or for learning. We all have that power. We must use it with care and love. I wish you the sound of children's laughter, the words of good news and the joy of music, and the turning your own good wishes to reality.

Epilogue

What is the conclusion of my life? I have gone through much hardship and many experiences, most of which I do not recommend to others. Suffering has made me realize the important values of life. The hardships have made every minute beyond them more precious and enjoyable. I am grateful for even the smallest things life has given me.

Most of us have difficulty in facing our inevitable end, and I am no exception. Goodbyes are hard. I never said goodbye to those I loved, even when the Nazis took me from my home. I can still see my father as he waved to me for the last time.

So back to that ancient Chinese curse—"I wish you an interesting life." I have had an interesting life, and some of the curses have become blessings. Indeed, I can say that I have had a hell of a good life; it has given me more than I have given back. I'd like to say more, but the time has come to put a period to the end.

We can never say everything we wish. When I was a little boy, I heard a fairy tale about a king who was looking for a suitable young man to marry his daughter and be his successor. He asked all the candidates to solve this puzzle: "Bring me a gift, and do not bring me a gift." No one seemed to have the answer. Years passed, and finally a young man arrived with a pigeon in his hand. As he handed it to the king, the young man let the bird fly away.

Life is the most precious gift we ever receive or can give, and like the bird, it flies away almost as we receive it. When young children with terminal illnesses want to share their fears with someone, they choose strangers— hospital workers—and talk with them at night. Why don't they talk with their parents? Because parents often do not want to discuss or accept a child's death, they deny it— yet the children know.

My advice is this: send the message—in time! We must all express how we feel, especially to those we love. I did not dare to say goodbye to my father because I was afraid, almost certain, that we would never see each other again. I do not want to repeat that mistake. I wish to hold the hands of my daughter, my friends, and my patients and recite to them the beautiful Hungarian folksong that was my grandmother's favorite:

> I'll come back to your mind
> while watching the stars in the sky;
> you wish to say once more hi,
> but then it will be too late.

We often do not have the time, the courage, or the opportunity to share all that is within us. Some of us are inhibited; others think no one will care. Sometimes we care too late. Think of the sad conclusion of Fellini's film *La Strada*—the strong, crude man of the circus collapses on the seashore under the stars, recognizing his failed and wasted life, neither understanding nor understood.

One Valentine's Day I watched as a mail carrier emptied a mailbox. Because of that special day, the box was stuffed to overflowing, and many pieces of mail fell to the ground. The mailman angrily picked them up and said, "I hate Valentines." A mailman who hates Valentines!

I feel fortunate that whatever I have done, even in times and places not of my choice, I have always enjoyed my work. The work itself and my belief in its importance—not any financial consideration—was my primary goal. I have always preferred idealism to practicality, and despite the difficulties, things eventually have worked out very well. The attitude with which we approach a choice, not the choice, makes the difference.

To be satisfied requires ability, desire, and opportunity; all these, denied when I was younger, eventually have been given to me. Different circumstances create different opportunities; we just need the eyes to recognize them.

Growing is a requirement for survival. An endless desire for knowledge and joy is part of life. The universe is constantly extending and changing, and we are part of it. We make every effort to avoid pain or even minimal discomfort. But how can we appreciate joy without knowing suffering? Suffering is a part of the learning experience. Suffering has made me appreciate everyday existence.

We cannot avoid suffering, but for the person who makes it through, there is an added dimension. Faith and love make it easier to go through a stormy, difficult time. I regret having lost the first of these (my faith), but I feel sorry for those who have had neither. When I was young, I enjoyed life; now I value it as well. Fear of life is more pitiful than fear of death.

I wonder about many things. What if I had been born a German and my father had been a high-ranking Nazi? Or a Russian and a Communist? Would I have stood up for them or against them? What if I had never been born and never experienced sorrow, laughter, light, colors, music, and human touch? We should never waste a minute of the precious gift we have.

But we cannot turn the clock back. We have limited choices and these are what we must use to the utmost. Like the Buddhists, we must try to achieve a better existence—not in another life but now! The only real change we can expect is a change in ourselves.

Life is like a rough diamond; we have an opportunity and a responsibility to polish it. Its light will show the way for us and maybe for others. If it is not cared for, even a diamond (because it is a carbon product) may burn in the flicker of time and disappear without a trace. We hope that when our children and friends look at the sky on starry nights, they will remember us not with sorrow for untold stories but with joy and gratitude for the warm, beautiful words, songs, and memories we have left behind.

When I see mothers leaving the hospital with their newborns, I always remind them of how long the nights are and how short life is. When I was young, I imagined a never-ending wall separating us from the unknown. We often hear someone say, "I am a survivor." In fact we are all survivors, until we die.

We carry with us our pasts—the gifts of those we love influence our lives as long as we live. The beginning for some is the end for others; each of us eventually becomes only a memory. My father lives as long as I do. And if I remain in only a single heart and mind, my life will have been worth living.

Robert O. Fisch is a native of Budapest, Hungary, and a survivor of the Holocaust. Following the war he returned to Hungary and completed medical school. In 1956 he was an active participant in the revolution against Communist suppression. For his heroism the Hungarian government awarded him a medal in 1995 and a knighthood in 2000.

Photo courtesy of Saari – Forrai Photography

Dr. Fisch escaped from Hungary and came to America. Shortly thereafter he became a medical intern at the University of Minnesota and was professor of pediatrics there from 1979 until his retirement in 1997. Fisch is known internationally for his clinical research in phenylketonuria (PKU), a genetic disease.

In addition to being a physician, he is also an artist who has studied at the Academy of Fine Arts in Budapest, the Minneapolis College of Art and Design, the University of Minnesota and the Walker Art Center. His artwork has won many awards.

Dr. Fisch's first book, *Light from the Yellow Star; A Lesson of Love from the Holocaust*, is an eloquent portrayal of his Holocaust experience. His message focuses on the importance of the human spirit and love that led the way for the survivors. The original paintings with the text have been exhibited in the United States, Europe and Israel, and the book itself is widely distributed in schools in the United States [by the Yellow Star Foundation (*yellostarfoundation.org*)] and Hungary.

Dr. Fisch wrote and illustrated *The Metamorphosis to Freedom* as a testimonial to freedom, the value he treasures above all others. Having survived the two most oppressive regimes of the 20th Century, he is eminently qualified to write about the quest for freedom.

Dear Dr. Fisch: Children's Letters to a Holocaust Survivor is a collection selected from thousands of letters he has received from American and European students who have heard his message. The letters are filled with love, humor, idealism, common sense and gratitude.

Artwork from *The Metamorphosis to Freedom* and *Dear Dr. Fisch* have been exhibited in Minnesota.